A Picture of
HAMPSHIRE

The Abbey Gate, Beaulieu, New Forest

A Picture of
HAMPSHIRE

by
JOHN L. BAKER

ROBERT HALE · LONDON

©John L. Baker 1986
First published in Great Britain 1986

ISBN 0 7090 2575 0

Robert Hale Limited
Clerkenwell House
Clerkenwell Green
London EC1

Baker, John L.
    A picture of Hampshire.
    1. Architecture——England——Hampshire
    I. Title
    720′.9422′7   NA969.H2

ISBN 0-7090-2575-0

Set in Palatino by
Kelly Typesetting Ltd., Bradford-on-Avon, Wiltshire
Printed in Great Britain by St. Edmundsbury Press,
Bury St. Edmunds, Suffolk
and bound by WBC

CONTENTS

To Jim Oliver, who shared with me his
knowledge of and deep affection for
Hampshire.

List of illustrations

Acknowledgements

Many friends have given me their time and valuable advice unstintingly. I particularly thank those who have read passages from my manuscript, the comments made by Dr E. Clive Rouse, MBE, FSA and Dr June Chatfield, B.Sc., Ph.D., ARCS, curator of the Oates Museum and the Gilbert White Museum, being greatly appreciated.

Many of the buildings mentioned are private property and it must be stressed that the privacy of owners must be respected at all times; the mention of a house in this book does not necessarily mean that it is open to the public.

For permission to make drawings I am grateful to the National Trust; the Dean of Winchester; the Department of the Environment, Ancient Monuments and Historic Buildings; the Master of St Cross; the curator of the Oates Museum and the Gilbert White Museum; the Warden and Fellows of Winchester College; and the headmaster of Twyford School.

For undertaking the task of typing my manuscript I thank my daughter Victoria, who laboured with the arduous task over a period of several months.

Finally I thank my wife for bearing with me over many months of intensive work and travel.

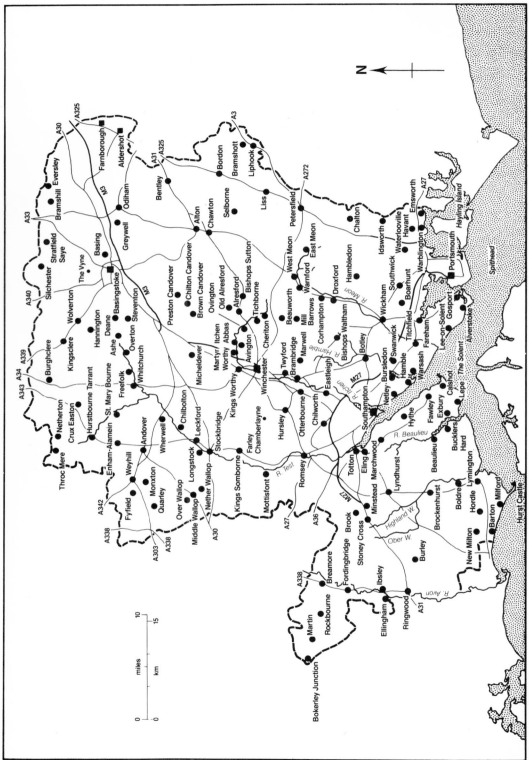

Hampshire

INTRODUCTION

John Ruskin records in Volume IV *Modern Painters*, in a foot-
note to Chapter Fifteen, that in response to a complaint by a
fellow artist that a landscape 'looked different' when he returned
to it, J.M.W. Turner, RA, the master of English landscape
painting, replied, 'What do you not know yet, at your age, that
you only paint an impression?' *A Picture of Hampshire* is my
impression, conveyed in words and drawings and offered
trusting that those who know the county intimately will find it a
worthy representation, and that those who seek to know it
better will find assistance in having the corner of the veil lifted
to reveal a glimpse of the county's wealth of history and
splendour of landscape.

Numbered with the larger English counties Hampshire, or
more correctly the County of Southampton, is well known for
broad downland, distant vistas and wide expanses of sky. This
however represents less than a third of the total area and
corresponds to a strata of chalk, in places some hundreds of
feet thick, which at or near the surface forms a band extending
across the county from Salisbury Plain to the North and South
Downs of Surrey and Sussex. A gradual upward slope of the
chalk towards the north-west produces the superb high country
around Linkenholt and Faccombe. Only partly within Hampshire, overrunning the county boundary and Fosbury, Butter-
mere and Combe, these chalk uplands form the southern
escarpment of the valley of the Kennet and its tributary the
Enborne, and extend eastwards to overlook the gravel and clays
which are drained by the Kennet before entering the Thames.

To the south where the chalk slides beneath the Tertiary
covering of the Hampshire Basin the landscape is as beautiful, if
less dramatic, as in the north-west. Seen at its finest at Butser,
and at Old Winchester Hill within the mass of the chalk, it is
especially gentle where the Rivers Test, Itchen and Meon flow
southward through wide valleys in the folds of the downs. The

13

chalk appears again in an upward fold to form a ridge at Ports-down where a great panorama opens to embrace both the inland landscape and the Solent.

Within the eastern boundary of the county lies the western edge of the Weald, where upper and lower greensand, older than the chalk, appear at the surface. Remarkable landscapes at Stonor and Selborne, compared with Switzerland by some writers, are created by beech 'hangers' where the chalk descends precipitously to greensand rocks below. Upper greensand occurs again as an outcrop between Burghclere and Kingsclere—but with less drama.

The geological formation of the county creates the surprises which Hampshire provides in its landscapes and its vernacular architecture, for in these two aspects that which is above the surface depends upon that which is below.

Mainland Hampshire lacks high quality building stone, but mention must be made of the Isle of Wight which possessed excellent Tertiary freestone. Two varieties, Quarr and Binstead, were extensively used for important work. The Romans used the former at Portchester Castle and the Normans chose it for Winchester Cathedral and Romsey Abbey. William of Wykeham had Binstead stone transported from the island to build Winchester College, and earlier the Cistercians used it for the abbeys of Beaulieu and Netley. It has also been identified in many Saxon churches throughout the county. Unfortunately both these stones were worked out by the late Middle Ages and their appearance in later work indicates re-use. Green ventnor, a greensand from Bonchurch and a good freestone, found favour in the Middle Ages, and although possibly a better stone, it is not of as much interest to us in the present context as the upper greensand at the western rim of the Weald which was once quarried in the region of Selborne. Known as 'malmstone' it is light-cream in colour, and although it did not attain the popularity of related sandstones quarried in Surrey and Sussex—such as Reigate stone—it was used at Winchester Castle and much may be seen in and near Selborne, especially at The Wakes. Another light-cream upper greensand was quarried near Kingsclere.

Lower greensand is a hard, coarse stone, brownish in colour according to the extent of its impregnation with iron oxide. Known as 'carstone', rarely quarried as large blocks but more frequently in pieces an inch or two thick, it is used as nogging in framed buildings. It shows to good effect set on edge for paving and is useful for galleting.

14

Sarsen stones, also called greyweathers or heathstones, are used little in the county as a building stone but may be seen at Compton and Eversley. They are sandstone boulders, products of an eroded strata of Tertiary sandstone, and borne by melting glacial action many have come from a great distance further north. Their strangeness both in appearance and distribution earned them a name derived from the word 'Saracen', meaning 'foreigner'.

The commonest traditional building material found in the downland is flint. Knapped, but infrequently dressed, it is coursed to form a facing to rubble walls, with brick or stone not only adding necessary strength at openings and corners but providing a contrast in colour and texture. The old school at Itchen Stoke with walls entirely of flint is an exception.

A hard variety of chalk found favour for interior work, especially where carved detail was required. With an external facing of brick it was used for the construction of the silk mill at Whitchurch, while at Marshcourt, Lutyens used it both internally and externally with great success.

Known as cob, crushed chalk combined with straw and water to form a stiff mixture became a common material for the construction of walls for houses, farm buildings and boundary walls. Frequently without the use of shuttering, the material was built up a foot or two at a time by allowing a hardening period between layers. Used extensively until the early nineteenth century, its use was revived during the early decades of this century. Many cob buildings and boundary walls survive from the seventeenth century in good order, and with a traditional roof of thatch few examples of vernacular building are more picturesque.

Hampshire has no shortage of fine clays for brickmaking, as architecture demonstrates in the City of Winchester and at towns such as Alton, Alresford, Odiham, Petersfield and Fareham and the superb Glenthorne, of about 1690, at East Meon. With brickworks grouped on the clays bordering the chalk downland, the greatest activity was south of a line from Rowland's Castle through Bishop's Waltham and Chandler's Ford to Fordingbridge. Fareham, Brockenhurst and Beaulieu were all noted for their bricks, while Southampton had its own official brickmaker in the late sixteenth century.

The clay areas in the county are also favourable to oak woodland and a tradition of timber-framed building is found in Hampshire which is dependent upon a great wealth of oak woodland in these localities. Examples of cruck construction,

15

a technique developed for agricultural and domestic buildings and large and small structures, are being continually discovered. The fifty-six or so recorded in the county before 1981, in the CBA Research Report, number forty-two, have now been greatly exceeded. The use of the cruck does not penetrate to neighbouring Surrey, the county boundary oddly coinciding with a demarcation of its use—a fact that has not been satisfactorily explained. I refer to the 'true' cruck and am aware of the few known examples of base crucks in Surrey and Sussex.

The crown-post and collar purlin appears to have been in general use. Farley Chamberlayne church has the most lovely that I have seen, admirable for its appropriate scale and simple lines of construction, but not least for its colour—the silver-grey of ancient oak. Another fine example of high quality is in a small wing of Church Farm House, West Tytherley.

The butted—tenoned—side purlin construction with wind-braces seen in the chancel roof at Basingstoke parish church is dated 1464 and is structurally more advanced than the crown-post. It appears to have been much used, but was in turn superseded by the use of a through side purlin construction perhaps by the early sixteenth century—increased economy in the use of timber without loss of stability being the criterion.

The churches at Rotherwick, Hartley Wespall and Mattingley provide fine examples of roof types and demonstrate the high quality of timber construction attained.

1 Winchester Cathedral and Precincts

A portrait of Hampshire must, I am sure, start with Winchester: a city that once surpassed London in the history of our nation; a city that was the capital of Wessex and of England; the place of burial of our early kings, Kynegils, Edgar, Alfred and Canute. In 1069 the Old Minster was the scene of William the Conqueror's second coronation, for he made Winchester joint capital with London and throughout his reign he 'wore his crown' in the city during the great festivals.

The visible signs of English architectural achievement are to be seen in abundance. Winchester College, the Hospital of St Cross, the Great Hall and Wolvesey Palace—these are of the highest importance, and there is street upon street of superb buildings that alone would make any city memorable. Added to this is the cathedral, remarkable both in its history and its architecture.

The value of the site upon which Winchester stands has been appreciated since ancient times. The Celts may have had a small settlement there, later developed by the Romans and named *Venta Belgarum*, which, following the subjection of south-east Britain by Vespasian was a meeting of important routes: six main roads radiated from it, and it had a status little less than that of Silchester. The Roman rectangular road grid is reflected in the modern plan, evidence suggests that a forum existed to the north of the cathedral, and the foundations of large houses have been found.

In the second half of the fourth century, invasions of Britain by Germanic tribes followed the decline of Roman influence and the area we now call Hampshire was settled by a people dedicated to farming who first occupied *Venta Belgarum*, before creating village communities along the river valleys. In AD 635 Pope Honorius I sent Birinus to evangelize the south and west of Britain. He landed at Southampton and was allowed to travel to

Winchester Cathedral: the north transept

John L. Baker

Dorchester on Thames where, in 635, he baptized Kynegils, King of the West Saxons, his son Kenwalh and many chiefs. Agreement was reached in the presence of Oswald, King of Northumbria, that Dorchester should be the 'bishopstool' until Kynegils 'could build in the royal city (Winchester) a temple worthy of so great a priest'. Kynegils died in 643, and Birinus, also, died before the transfer of the 'bishopstool' in 676 to a new church built by Kenwalh in Winchester—parent of the Old Minster and the cathedral we see today.

Egbert became King of Wessex in 802 and assumed supremacy over the north as 'King of Angleland'. Thus Winchester may be claimed to be the first capital of England. Swithun, venerated in his time and later canonized, was appointed to the bishopric in 852, and for ten years his episcopate was memorable for his piety and humility, also for his vigour as a builder of churches. The precinct walls owe their origin to him.

Alfred the Great came to the kingship in 871 when England was greatly harassed by the Danes, but in 878 he made peace at Wedmore in Somerset with the Dane Guthrum and England became divided. Roman Watling Street became the boundary between northern, central and eastern England, held by the Danes and known as the Danelaw, and Alfred's Saxon kingdom of Wessex with Winchester as capital.

A period of peace and artistic activity followed. Alfred initiated the writing of *The Chronicle*—the first history book—and many other books were produced, including a translation of Gregory's *Pastoral Code* from Latin into West Saxon. Following Alfred's death, his son Edward the Elder carried out his father's wish and, north of the Old Minster, built the New Minster where ultimately he and his father were buried.

Bishop Ethelwold initiated religious reform in 963 when he introduced the Benedictine Rule and rebuilt the Old Minster. During the reign of Alfred's son Edward, Bishop Grimbald had brought the miracle-working relics of St Josse to the New Minster—Ethelwold required a similarly beneficial saint for the Old Minster. He therefore translated the body of St Swithun to a shrine in the minster, but his disregard of St Swithun's dying wish to be buried in the churchyard in 'a vile and unworthy place', together with a violent thunderstorm, gave rise to the superstition associated with rain on St Swithun's Day. Literary and other artistic work continued and the Winchester School of Illumination flourished.

Cnut was elected king by the Witan at Southampton in 1016 and later became king over all England bringing a period of quiet government. Following his death a division of interests occurred, brought about by Norman influences introduced by Cnut's Norman wife Emma and later by her grandson, Edward the Confessor.

With victory at Hastings, William was welcomed in Winchester Cathedral for his second coronation in 1068, but retribution descended upon the Saxon Bishop Stigand, who was described as covetous and unscrupulous and was accused of holding the bishoprics of Winchester and Canterbury in plurality. The bishop's career ended in ignominy and the monks of the New Minster who had clung to the Saxon cause fared little better: with part of their abbey precinct taken for the Conqueror's Palace, they lost their revenues and were denied an abbot.

Walkelin, cousin of William, was inducted as bishop, and in 1079 he began rebuilding the Old Minster, resited to the south at an angle to Bishop Ethelwold's edifice so that the western end passed across the line of the old nave, which was taken down as work advanced. On 8 April 1093 the relics of St Swithun were translated to a shrine in the new building.

The plan of the Norman cathedral was almost the same as that of the cathedral we see today. Walkelin's building had an apsidal east end, the original Norman work to be found in the apsidal crypt being assumed to have corresponded with work above. At the west end the nave extended further westward and terminated with large twin towers.

Although Walkelin's plan is almost unchanged, all the Norman elevations have been modified, or rebuilt, except the north and south transepts. The tower is Norman, but it was rebuilt in 1200 after it had collapsed in 1107. The later style betrays its date in the type of decoration used and the precise workmanship of the stonemasons. The transepts alone give an impression of the plain, uncompromising early Norman style in which the whole cathedral was first built. In the unusual construction of these transepts at their respective north and south extremities, there is an indication that corner towers were intended but later abandoned due to the unstable nature of the marshy site.

During the late twelfth century Bishop Godfrey de Lucy initiated the building of the retrochoir, with a Lady chapel flanked by chapels to the north and south. It was to be a fitting place for the shrine of St Swithun, with access from the nave provided by walkways on both sides of the choir. Admission was through the wrought-iron gate—the oldest grille-work in England—still known as the Pilgrim Gate. De Lucy died in 1202 before the work was completed, but he instituted a 'confraternity

Winchester Cathedral: the west end of the south aisle showing the contrasting work of Bishop Edington and Bishop Wykeham

for the reparation of the church of Winton, to last for five years'.

De Lucy's glorious Early English retrochoir remains, but the Lady Chapel was extended eastward and remodelled in the fifteenth century. It contains early sixteenth-century wall paintings executed in brown and grey representing the miracles of the Blessed Virgin, appreciation of which is assisted by modern reproductions painted on folding screens by Professor Tristram FSA. The south-east chapel was remodelled by Bishop Langton as his chantry. The north-east chapel, dedicated to the 'Guardian Angels' with thirteenth-century paintings of angels on the vault, contains the tomb of Richard Weston, Duke of Portland, who died in 1634. It is an outstanding classical composition with a bronze effigy by Le Sueur.

The work of remodelling the choir begun in 1320 was completed by Bishop Fox, who built the side aisles with vaults of wood around 1510. Fortunately his intention to transform the eastern aisles of the transepts was not realized. In 1525 he erected the stone side screens of the choir which support wooden tomb-chests of Anglo-Saxon kings.

The most dramatic and important change to the fabric of the cathedral commenced under the direction of Bishop Edington in the last years of his episcopate. Stonework at the west end had deteriorated and Edington dismantled the Norman west front with its twin towers and shortened the nave by one bay. He then closed the truncated nave with a new west front in the decorated style, but died in 1366 before he could complete the great west window and the flanking turrets. Ziegler, in *The Black Death* (1969), wrote that Edington 'threw up' the west front 'in a hurry' and at low cost, and this must describe the mood of the times with the Black Death at its destructive zenith in Hampshire during 1348-9.

Edington's mason is unknown, but William of Wykeham, his successor at Winchester, took up the work in 1394 with William de Wynford, the King's Mason, as Clerk of Works, and continued remodelling the nave in the newly evolved Perpendicular style until his death in 1404. Bishop Beaufort continued, followed by Bishop Waynflete.

As described by the Reverend R. Willis in his paper 'The Architectural History of the Cathedral', 1846, the transformation of the interior was achieved by cutting back existing Norman masonry and removing the triforium to allow tall arcade arches and large clerestory windows with only a narrow panelled parapet carried on a corbelled frieze between them. The overall height was unchanged and corresponds with the unaltered transepts. This was in the style current at the time, and named 'Perpendicular' by Thomas Rickman in his book on architecture, published in 1819.

The story of how Bishop Walkelin acquired the timber for his Norman cathedral roof may be untrue but it is worth retelling. The King offered the bishop as much timber from Hampage Wood as he could take in three days—or a day and a night, versions vary—not expecting that the wily bishop would muster a small army of woodcutters and haulers to remove the whole wood. I have been privileged to enter the spaces above the vaults to see the roofs (and an exciting experience it proved to be) and I wondered if any of the Hampage oak could be identified. Unfortunately there are no complete roof structures that could be as early as 1079, although the end of a tiebeam 'stonefast' in the nave wall has been noted (Hewett 1980) and could be Norman.

A section of the nave roof may belong to the period of William de Wynford when he remodelled the nave in the late fourteenth century, but the western end of the nave has a documented date—1699. The presbytery roof is above work instigated by Bishop Fox in the first half of the sixteenth century when wooden vaulting was inserted—earlier work below in this area dates from the early fourteenth century, and the roof has been dated from this period.

The north transept was ceiled with suspended wooden panelling in the nineteenth century, which concealed a complex roof similar in type to the presbytery roof, and hid the rose window in the north gable, which was Prior Silkstede's work. But the south transept roof may be compared to the late fourteenth century section above the nave and may well be the oldest of the cathedral roofs.

Winchester Cathedral from the south-west

Despoliation at Winchester during the Dissolution proved less disastrous than at other religious foundations. Thomas Cromwell's Commission arrived in 1538. They destroyed the shrine, removed jewels and other valuables, but a compromise was reached, and Winchester became a New Foundation administered not by an abbot, but by a dean assisted by prebendaries. The land, and the income from it, formerly owned by the Benedictines, was transferred to the New Foundation.

With the accession of Mary I came a brief revival of the old religion, and pageantry returned for the marriage of the Queen to Prince Philip of Spain on 25 July 1554. Tapestries recently completed in Flanders for Philip and diverted to England decorated the nave—the hooks that supported them may be seen in the piers of the nave arcade. A further reminder of the occasion is the chair used by the Queen during the ceremony, now in the chantry of Bishop Gardiner, who conducted the service.

Within a few years of the death of Mary the monastic buildings were either demolished or converted to secular use. There followed a respite until 1642, when the bigotry of the Cromwellian period resulted in great damage to the cathedral, with the smashing of all the stained glass windows and carvings. There is no limit to the unthinking, blind ignorance of those possessed with 'religion'.

Despite two destructive forays into the cathedral, much of interest and beauty still remains. The chantries, complete in sequence of the medieval and Tudor bishops of the diocese, taken together form an illustrated history of English architecture, each being built, regardless of expense, in the fashion of the time.

The styles of the Edington and Wykeham chantries reflect their work in the remodelled nave. The elaborate Beaufort chantry shows an effigy of the cardinal beneath a fan vault—the earliest in the cathedral—and a statue of Joan of Arc, with the faintest trace of a serene smile stands nearby facing one of her judges. Bishop Fox died in 1528 and his chantry remains Gothic, but Bishop Gardiner's, who died in 1555, shows Renaissance influence.

The magnificent choir has finely carved stalls. They date from 1308 but are late thirteenth century in style, in that the seats have misericords carved with a variety of amusing incidents. The pulpit dating from 1520 carries a rebus—a silk skein—of Prior Silkstede, in its exceptionally elaborate carving. Centrally placed nearby is the tomb of William Rufus. The reredos of Cardinal Beaufort's time, or a little later, is of stone, and arranged in three tiers of canopied niches flanking a central panel containing the Crucifixion, it extends to above the sills of the clerestory windows. Although badly damaged by Cromwellian soldiers, restoration in the nineteenth century replaced the statues and brought back much of its original beauty. The superb canopies are original.

The Chapel of the Holy Sepulchre contains a series of wall-paintings of the mid-thirteenth century, important to scholars as they reflect the work of the Winchester Scriptorium. The Pantocrator is shown in the eastern spandrel above a scene showing Christ taken from the Cross, below Christ placed in the tomb, and angels in rondels look down from the vault above. The chapel, not a chantry, is used every Saturday—the day Christ lay in the tomb.

The Tournai 'marble' font brought to Winchester in the twelfth century shows scenes from the life of St Nicholas and is one of the four remaining in Hampshire churches and one of seven known to have been imported by an agent probably sponsored by Henry de Blois. It is of importance to students of naval history as one of the carvings provides the earliest known representation of a ship with a rudder.

Winchester Cathedral: detail of the font, showing a ship with a rudder

In the north aisle floor west of the font is a simple grave slab of Jane Austen, who was fittingly laid to rest at the heart of the county in which she lived and wrote some of the finest literature in the English language.

Although tribute is made to those who created Winchester Cathedral, one man with his own hands saved it from ruin. He was the naval diver William Walker. In 1905 the ground beneath the cathedral, waterlogged and marshy, would no longer support the building. Norman builders had constructed the cathedral on a raft of logs, and similar precautions were taken in the thirteenth century when building the east end. These rafts had sunk, and the south-east of the cathedral was in great danger. The engineer asked to advise was Sir Francis Fox, a descendant of Bishop Fox, and he insisted that the foundations be under-pinned down to hard gravel. Pumping water out of the foundations would increase the danger of collapse, so a diver was sought to descend into the black water and under-pin the foundations with thousands of bags of concrete, concrete blocks and bricks. William Walker laboured for six years under the cathedral, while above the walls were grouted where necessary and buttresses added to the south aisle of the nave where the greatest danger lay.

Precincts occupy the south-east quarter of the old city and contain the monastic buildings of the Priory at St Swithun, of which the present cathedral was the Priory Church. Excavation has revealed the sites of the Old and the New Minsters north of the cathedral and foundations of domestic buildings, probably belonging to the New Minster and dating from the early

A Benedictine monk

Norman period, have been found south of High Street near the Wessex Hotel. The cloister and monastic buildings, either in ruins or much altered, are south of the cathedral—the standard Benedictine arrangement.

The Chapter House, the monks' dormitory and the Deanery are in line with the south transept on the eastern side of the site of the cloister. The ruins of the Chapter House, contemporary with the transepts isolated and out of context, are not so much impressive as intimidating—the massive double-scalloped capitals say more about the Normans than any number of words in a history book. South of the Chapter House the Prior's House, now the Deanery, is exceptionally fine, comparable to Bishop de Lucy's retrochoir of the early thirteenth century.

The Deanery, Winchester Cathedral Close

Possibly the most interesting building in the precinct, known as the Pilgrims Hall, abuts the Pilgrims School attended by the cathedral choristers. The original purpose of this building is unknown, but in the seventeenth century the hall was a brew-house, and after 1660 it was used by the dean as a coach-house and stable with a hayloft above. Restored in 1959 and the hayloft removed, the floor was lowered to its supposed original level, and a stage put in for the use of the school. The hall became known as the Pilgrims Hall on the supposition that it provided accommodation for large numbers of pilgrims to the shrine of St Swithun—a reasonable assumption, but one without documentary foundation. However, the unusual arrangement of the building has not, so far, given clues to its original purpose. The roof has two hammer-beam trusses with the ends of the hammer-beams carved with kings' or bishops' heads. Such carvings on the end grain of the beam are rare—perhaps unique. During the

Cheyne Court, Winchester Cathedral Close

visit to Winchester of the Royal Archaeological Institute in 1845, it was dated to the reign of Edward I: dendrochronology has estimated 1324-30. It is the earliest domestic hammer-beam roof identified—a roof of similar construction at Westminster Hall, London, dates from 1392-9, and only the hammer-beams in the octagon at Ely Cathedral are a few years earlier.

East of Pilgrims School is Wolvesey Castle, the Bishop's Palace. A complex of buildings containing the residence of the Bishops of Winchester since the twelfth century, it has early work attributed to Henry de Blois that includes a ruined gatehouse, a first-floor hall, and a keep. The old buildings were occupied until Bishop Morley's addition of 1684, which has been tenuously attributed to Wren.

Morley seems to have been a caring bishop. In 1672 he established Morley College, an almshouse for ministers' widows, still on the north-west side of the precinct, but rebuilt in 1880. He also left his library to the dean and chapter. It formed the nucleus of the present cathedral library, which contains some three or four thousand books and rare manuscripts, the most valuable being *The Vulgate*, dating from the twelfth century, perhaps the finest extant example of the art of the Winchester School.

2 Winchester—The City

With sword held high, King Alfred looks upon his ancient capital from a monolith in the Broadway. He might reflect upon the changes that have taken place, or perhaps upon the truth of the words of Richard of Devizes in 1198, 'Winchester does nothing in a hurry, fears nothing so much as having to repent at leisure, counts the end more than the beginning'. (Kitchen 1907).

King Alfred the Great by Hamo Thornycroft

Hamo Thornycroft's statue of Alfred erected in 1901 stands near the site of the Nunnaminster, recently excavated in the Guildhall Gardens and car-park. Founded by Alfred and his Queen, the Nunnaminster was a house of Benedictine nuns, and with the Old Minster and the New Minster it was one of the most important religious houses in the city. The grouping of these three great Saxon churches with conventual buildings clustered around them would have been an exciting architectural spectacle, picturesque in its variety and made exciting by the imaginative constructional techniques of Saxon masons.

The Guildhall nearby, in a late-nineteenth century Gothic style, and recently cleaned, is an asset adding interest and colour to the Broadway. Westwards along High Street, now a pedestrian precinct, a variety of handsome buildings may be seen, including the Old Guildhall, with a great clock given in 1713 by Sir William Paulet. Once open at ground level with the first floor supported on Tuscan columns, it was closed with shop fronts in the nineteenth century, but from the heavy louvred cupola the Conqueror's curfew is still rung at eight every evening. The statue of Queen Anne placed in a first-floor niche commemorates the Treaty of Utrecht.

The front of the jettied Godbegot House—a courtyard house opposite—has been restored. The building is sixteenth century and stands on the manor of Godbegot granted by Queen Emma to the Prior of St Swithun 'free of tolls and taxes for ever'. Within the confines of the manor law-breakers obtained sanctuary and were accountable only to the Prior.

The office of one of the oldest of the county's newspapers the *Hampshire Chronicle*, established in 1772, stands opposite. A handsome front with bow windows pre-dates the newspaper by a generation.

The Butter Cross, erected at a point where the paved way widens, dates from the early fifteenth century. Repaired for the marriage of Mary I in July 1554 and then thoroughly restored by Scott in 1865, it was nearly lost to the city in 1770 when a proposal to sell it to Mr Dummer to re-erect as a folly in Cranbury Park was frustrated at the last minute. The pillarbox near the cross stands close to the site of the old town pump and the houses grouped behind on the site of the tenements 'Hevyn' and 'Helle' and 'Bulhall' contain ancient work. Panelling— some linenfold—may be seen in the house extending over the pavement, and although the exterior looks eighteenth century the structure contains much older work. The jettied and gabled house behind the cross has a wooden window with a row of four ogee lights, said to be fourteenth century.

31

Offices of the Hampshire Chronicle

In a square near the museum at the back of these properties stood a cage and a pillory. Also in Minster Street, is St Laurence Church probably dating from the thirteenth century, altered and restored. Referred to as the 'Mother Church', it occupies the site of the chapel in the Conqueror's Palace which is now gone. Before his enthronement a bishop is received by the dignitaries of the city in St Laurence, and after prayers he is invested with his episcopal robes by the archdeacon.

Number 105 in the High Street, once the house of George Earle, an apothecary, is dated 1772 and is a superb house by any standards. It is at the point where the pedestrian way ceases and the road continues up hill to the Westgate, a thirteenth-century gate of the city. The west side is of later date and has imposing machicolations and two early gunports which once gave authenticity to its defensive capabilities, but with road widening, and the removal of property on its northern flank, it has lost conviction as a defensive work. It houses a museum containing the standard weights and measures fixed by the Tudor sovereigns.

Within the gate are excavated sections of fortifications begun by the Normans in 1067 and extended and improved by sub-sequent English kings. William I, conscious of the political importance of the city, had regard for its fortification and strengthened the castle. The Royal Treasury was kept at Winchester well into the twelfth century, and the administrative facilities in the city were such that the Domesday Book named in its pages 'the book of Winchester', which was compiled and kept there.

The castle was the birthplace of Henry III in 1207, also of Prince Arthur, son of Henry VII. In 1522 Henry VIII chose to meet Charles of Germany and Spain at Winchester and, anxious to impress a rival prince, he entertained him in great splendour in the Great Hall of the castle. Charles I garrisoned the castle during the Civil War, but, taken by Cromwell in 1645 and slighted, only the Great Hall survived.

After the Restoration, Charles II commissioned Wren to build a new palace and grandiose plans were made for a large Renaissance house which would have surpassed Hampton Court, but, uncompleted before the King's death, James II did not continue the work. The unfinished house, which was used as a barracks and destroyed by fire in 1894, was rebuilt as a depot for the Royal Green Jackets.

Following the destruction of an earlier building by the French in 1216, a master mason called Stephen rebuilt the Great Hall of

The east face of Winchester Westgate

the castle between 1222 and 1236. Aisled with arcade piers, each having eight detached Purbeck marble shafts with round moulded abaci, the pointed arches of the tall, delicately moulded arcades give a light, airy character to the interior. The dais placed at the west end was below three small lancet windows high in the gable, and a doorway at this end led to the solar. Original doorways in the north and south walls can be identified, although the entrance is now through a central doorway of Victorian date. The eaves line was raised and the roof replaced in 1873.

A statue of Queen Victoria by Alfred Gilbert, commissioned to celebrate her Diamond Jubilee in 1897 and now in the hall, formerly stood in Abbey Gardens. An outstanding example of late-nineteenth century art, executed with extraordinary skill, it would repay thought and imagination in providing a more worthy setting either in the present building or elsewhere.

The round table in the hall, the subject of much deliberation concerning its age, remains a mystery. The painting on it is a repainting of 1522, done for the meeting of Charles V of Germany and Spain with Henry VIII, but the earliest documented date of mention is in the 1360s when it was then 'of great age'.

From early times until recently, courts of Assize and Quarter Sessions were held in the hall and the cruellest trial known to have taken place there was during Judge Jeffreys' 'Bloody Assize', when he forced a guilty verdict on Dame Alice Lisle and condemned her to the fire, only reducing the sentence to beheading after pressure had been brought to bear.

Jewry Street recalls the presence of Jews in the city where they were encouraged to settle following the Conquest. They continued to be well received, a massacre occurring only once in 1265 by Simon de Montfort the Younger, not by the citizens, of whom it was said that in all England, 'Winchester is for the Jews the Jerusalem of that land'. Jews, expelled from the kingdom in 1290 during the reign of Edward I, were engaged in the business of moneylending forbidden to Christians. They were necessary to the nobles until the Italians—Florentines and Siennese known by the name of 'Lombards'—took their place.

In Jewry Street two surviving wings of the Old Gaol built in 1805 in stock brick by G. Moneypenny have vermiculated quoins, and the Corn Exchange—now the County Library, built by O.B. Carter in 1836—is an impressive composition, the centre not a little influenced by St Paul's of Covent Garden, London. A contrast to its conventional formality is provided by an extravaganza in chinoiserie, 'The Pagoda' in Romsey Road, built in 1848-9 by Richard Andrews. A walk up the hill to see it is rewarding.

New Minster, later known as Hyde Abbey, was founded in 901 by Edward, son of Alfred the Great, to fulfil his father's wishes and stood on land north of the Old Minster given by Alfred before his death. The remains of Alfred were buried in the New Minster, and later the body of Alfred's wife, foundress of the Nunnaminster. The abbey fell on bad times during the reign of Rufus and difficulties arose through overcrowding and closeness to the Old Minster—it is said that the monks' singing in the two Minsters became intermingled and confused. Relief came by the will of Abbot Geoffrey, and the monks were able to move in 1109 from the old site to Hyde Mead, north of the city, where to their new house known as Hyde Abbey they took their sacred relics, including 'the great gold cross of Cnut's benefaction' and the remains of King Alfred.

In April 1538, with the monastery surrendered and the grave of Alfred destroyed, Leland reported that he could find nothing but the site, for the monastic buildings were reduced to ruin.

The Gatehouse survives in King Alfred Place off Hyde Street.

During the seventeenth and eighteenth centuries town houses were built in St Peter's Street and Parchment Street between St George's Street and North Walls. Avebury House in St Peter's Street dates from 1690. Number four and the Royal Hotel are late seventeenth century. In Parchment Street, number nine has a fine door-hood with elaborately carved brackets, and inside a good staircase.

East of this area, Upper, Middle, and Lower Brook Street, and Friarsgate up to the Broadway, was the working quarter of the town, where tradesmen and craftsmen had their shops. It is still a pleasant, busy area, not entirely lost in new development. A craftsman's house, that of a lead merchant and plumber, has been preserved in Middle Brook Street.

The River Itchen flows along the eastern border of the city beneath the City Mill, built in 1774 of brick with tile-hanging and now serving as a youth hostel. Crossed by Bridge Street, carried on a single span bridge dated 1813, the river flows southward past the gardens of property bordering Chesil Street to skirt the grounds of Wolvesey Castle. From Bridge Street, St John's Street climbs steeply northward past the church of St John the Baptist, which has a fifteenth-century tower built into the hillside as if to buttress the remainder of the church. This was used by the scholars of Winchester College on Sundays and Feast Days, when the School was on the lower slopes of St Giles Hill before the college was erected. With an exceptionally fine interior St John's has a late-twelfth-century arcade with large round piers, fourteenth-century parclose screens and a fifteenth-century rood screen across the chancel and the side chapels. A stair turret was entered from the east. Mortice holes in the roof timber above indicate the position of the rood. Thomas Ken, later Bishop of Winchester, preached from the fourteenth-century pulpit in 1672. Wall-paintings reported to have been found in 1852 were destroyed, but in 1958 more paintings dating from the thirteenth century were discovered on the splays of two lancet windows found in the north wall. A beautiful late thirteenth-century geometric window in the south wall of the south chapel may be seen to great advantage from the road.

Further up the hill the Blue Boar, a fourteenth-century jettied hall house, contains three interior galleries. One—possibly two—is genuine.

Chesil Street has many buildings of interest. The church of St Peter—now a theatre—has a fat tile-hung tower of the thirteenth century, to the north of which stands a group of eighteenth-

A superb door-hood in Parchment Street, Winchester

A busy shopping day in Winchester

century houses and also Chesil Rectory, a twin-gabled and jettied timber-framed house with long curving braces and carved barge-boards. The name Chesil, or Cheesehill, came from the gravel bank, or chesil, bordering the river, where boats from Southampton were loaded and unloaded. Chesil Street is within the Liberty of the Soke, which comprised an area outside East Gate together with certain property within the city and was administered by the bishop's bailiff and sergeants, monies from rents and taxes providing a considerable income. St Giles Fair, another large source of income for the bishop, flourished in Bishop Walkelin's time when William Rufus granted him a fair on the Feast of St Giles—in September—to be held on the hill east of the city. It was possibly the first, and for many years one of the largest, fairs of its kind to be held in England. It drew traders from the Continent and the Mediterranean, even slowing down trade in London. The powers of the bishop at this time were extensive and irksome to the citizens of Winchester. Able to suspend all business activity in the city, he had his own 'Court of Pavilion' which dealt with legal matters arising from the fair, and the keys of the city, together with all powers, were handed over by the mayor and bailiffs to the bishop's seneschal for the sixteen day duration of the fair.

In the fourteenth century the Black Death greatly reduced activities, and by the fifteenth century the citizens of Winchester, smarting under the bishop's privileges and powers to meddle, obtained their own fair. Later, during the period of the Dissolution, the St Giles Fair and the Court of Pavilion ceased in their original form.

From Chesil Street a footpath alongside the Itchen leads to College Street and St Mary's College, one of the city's famous foundations. William of Wykeham became Bishop of Winchester in 1366, and his work on the cathedral with the master mason Wynford has been mentioned. He also envisaged founding a school at Winchester to complement New College Oxford, founded in 1369. The school was an independent ecclesiastical foundation with the approval of a Papal Bull of June 1378, the object being to produce an educated clergy—secular not monastic—to repair the depredations of the Black Death.

With the Charter executed on 20 October 1382, in the chapel of Winchester Palace, Southwark, building of the new College of St Mary began in 1387 on land purchased in the Soke outside the city. Thomas Cranley, afterwards Archbishop of Dublin, became the first warden, and seventy scholars were admitted. The school started in a building outside the East Gate on the

Winchester College

lower slopes of St Giles' Hill but moved to the new building on
28 March 1394, and the consecration of the chapel took place
on 17 July 1395.

The college survived the rigours of the Dissolution Acts of
Edward VI and similarly fared well during the Civil War. The
story is told of two Wykehamist parliamentary officers who
stood with swords drawn to prevent the desecration of Wykeham's chantry in the cathedral when all else was being defaced.
This may be apocryphal, but it expresses the position taken by
the college—a conditional sympathy with the Parliamentarians,
from whom they had little to fear.

From the small house where Jane Austen spent her last days
in College Street a maze of narrow lanes with attractive houses
leads from Kingsgate Street to Southgate Street lined with many
eighteenth-century houses in red brick, including Southgate
Hotel, dated 1715. Searle's house, an exceptional house of the
early eighteenth century—and early enough to have a baroque,
robust seventeenth-century appearance—has quadrant curves

Jane Austen's house in College Street, Winchester

bringing the centre boldly forward. Giant pilasters at each end of the façade and on either side of the projecting centre, support a pediment with curving parapet above. The house contains the Royal Hampshire Regimental Museum.

Southgate Street leads into the country to the ancient Hospital of St Cross, founded about 1133 by Henry de Blois, third Norman Bishop of Winchester. Papal Bulls confirmed the charter making provision for housing, clothing, and feeding 'thirteen poor impotent men, so reduced in strength as rarely or never to be able to raise themselves without the assistance of another'. In addition one hundred poor men of good conduct were to be fed daily at dinner. Dispute arose between Henry de Blois' successor and the Order of Hospitallers to whom the charter had been delivered. The Hospitallers surrendered management in 1185 and yielded to the bishop, who agreed that two hundred, instead of the original one hundred poor men should be fed daily. Disputes however, were not at an end and continued between the diocese and the Hospitallers. In 1204 a Papal Commission upheld the claims of the Bishop of Winchester—Godfrey de Lucy—who appointed a master, but bad management and dispute continued until Wykeham became bishop in 1368 and put an end to the wrangling. When he took control he found that the great hall had fallen in and the buildings for the thirteen brethren were uninhabitable. He bore down on the mismanagement of funds, began repairs to the buildings and made money available to administer the charity.

Bishop Wykeham died in 1404. Henry Beaufort, who followed him as bishop, wished to add a hospital of 'Noble Poverty' to the foundation: it is believed that the present lodgings and Brothers Great Hall were built by him about 1445, but he did not fully carry out his intentions before he died. It was left to Wynflete, his successor, to complete them, but again there appear to have been difficulties and Beaufort's plans for the additional almshouses of 'Noble Poverty' had to be completed in a greatly modified form in 1486. Instead of the intended thirty-five brethren, three sisters and two priests, there were two brethren and one priest. Scandal continued, only brought to a final conclusion in 1855-7 when the present equitable arrangements were devised.

There are twenty-five apartments available for a small rent, and the proportion of brothers is seventeen of the Henry de Blois foundation to eight of the Beaufort. The Henry de Blois brothers wear black gowns and a silver cross-potent emblem ordained by the Hospitallers. Claret gowns on which are embroidered in white a cardinal's hat and a small cross are worn by the Beaufort brothers. The conditions require beneficiaries to be men of sixty-five years of age or over, British subjects, members of the Church of England and in reasonably good health. The Master is always a clergyman.

The outer gate leads to the entrance court, bounded to the east by the Hundred Men's Hall and to the south by the Beaufort Tower, in which an archway gives access to a large inner quadrangle. This is formed by a western range containing the lodgings of the brethren, and to the north the Master's House, and the Great Hall alongside the Beaufort Tower. Built by Robert Sherborne, a Master in the late fifteenth century, a range once containing the infirmary closes the eastern side. The southern side, now partly formed by the nave of the chapel, was once closed by eight dwellings demolished in the nineteenth century.

Disputes in the twelfth and thirteenth centuries probably interfered with progress on the chapel, which was not completed until the mid-fourteenth century. As was the custom, building began at the east end. The chancel is Norman but as work progressed changes of style occurred. The chancel contains remarkable late Norman work, such as zigzag ornament

The quadrangle of the Hospital of St Cross, showing the Beaufort Tower and entrance porch to the Brethren's Hall

44

set at right angles to the wall which has a very unpleasant 'jazzy' appearance. More of this type of ornament may be seen in the south chapel, where the confusion caused by the transition to an Early English style is evident. The nave has massive arcade piers supporting pointed arches, but the western bays are entirely Early English in feeling.

William Butterfield applied colour to the walls and mouldings during his restoration in 1864-5. This has been removed, but a photograph in the *Victoria County History* shows the chancel as he left it—a black and white photograph, but enough to indicate that it would not be acceptable to modern taste.

The Brethren's Hall has a fine interior, containing tables which are original although the benches are not. The Summoning Bell, the Senior Brother's Chair and a Tudor linen-press may be seen, together with other items of interest, but the Alms Bowl is modern—the original having been stolen.

Known to date from within a year or two of 1445, the superb roof is of importance to historians as the construction is assumed to be unchanged, although the timber is not all original. Large arched braces stand on corbels formed as angels heads and meet beneath collar-beams near the apex of the principal rafters on each side. The roof contains three tiers of wind-braces with side purlins butted into the principal rafters, the upper wind-braces curving downwards from the principal rafters to the upper purlins. This roof is similar to one above the chancel at Basingstoke Parish Church dated 1464.

At the high end of the hall the Master's table stands on a dais from which a stair leads to the tower which was formerly the Master's lodging. At the opposite end, a screened cross-passage with a gallery above has entrances into the hall. One leads from the quadrangle—a grand entrance approached up steps—and there is another opposite leading from the service rooms and the kitchen in the north wing. Two doorways through the screen give access from the passage to the hall. The siting of the service rooms does not conform to the usual medieval plan in which they are beyond the cross-passage in line with the hall. In this position there are lodgings, which were later used by the Master who moved from the tower. The Master now lives in a Victorian house north of the Outer Gate. The positioning of the kitchen away from the hall was quite usual—to minimize fire risk.

In a most admirable guide entitled *Hampshire*, by J. Charles Cox and revised by R.L.P. Jowitt, it is written 'St Cross . . . the most beautiful group of medieval buildings yet remaining to us, was founded about 1133 by Bishop Henry de Blois.'

3   From Winchester to Southampton

From St Cross a modern road follows the line of the Roman Winchester to Bitterne road to Compton, then it, in turn, is overlaid and crossed by even newer roads which sweep down from the north and bypass Winchester to the east. Along this road the Old Contemptibles who assembled in southern England marched to war in 1914-18, and like many British armies before them their port of embarkation for France was Southampton. The wooden wayside cross above the road at Compton commemorates them. Another cross, one of stone on a hill nearby at Shawford, commemorates the men of the village who did not return from the First and Second World Wars. This locality seems an appropriate place for such memorials, for from the footpaths that lead across the hilltops there are extensive views across the countryside which symbolize the land those men died to defend.

These hills stand at the southern edge of the great band of chalk that extends across the county, and from them the Itchen flows southward, often dividing into numerous streams as it passes through a widening valley towards Southampton. A wooded landscape of chalk-loving beech trees mingles with the oak and pine of the clay and sand in the Hampshire Basin. The hills are not high, but rise sufficiently to produce a varied landscape, green and lush in the wide valley. The 'brick country' starts here—there is a Kiln Lane at Brambridge—and flint and brick are used together. Timber-framing may also be found and in addition there is a little heathstone (sarsen stone) in Compton church near the village school, a short distance from the main road. Enlargements to the church in 1904-5 included the addition of a new nave and chancel to the south, but much of the original twelfth-century work was preserved including small round-headed Norman windows in the north, south and west walls of the nave. One in the south wall retains

All Saints Church, Compton: the Norman nave and chancel

original fastenings for a shutter. The Norman north door also remains the best architectural feature of that date. The chancel, which maybe dates from the twelfth century, has a fourteenth century east window and two windows in the north wall are earlier lancets. A mural painting on the eastern splay of the north-east window depicts a bishop with a crosier. An inscription has been deciphered, naming him *S Theoph . . . nus.*

From Compton a narrow road below the war memorial, leads past Shawford railway station and across the valley to Twyford, through a landscape enhanced by glimpses of the tall tower and spire of Twyford church. New housing developments reach out across the valley from Twyford village street, now as the A333 made unpleasant and dangerous by fast-moving traffic. However, unless field paths across the valley are taken, the A333 has to be negotiated to reach the church which stands near the top of the valley side on a site that offers all an architect could desire. The steeple of the church is silhouetted against the sky even in a distant prospect and the foreground of river and meadows could not be more picturesque. In 1876 Alfred Waterhouse demolished the old church—perhaps much of it twelfth century. Only the late twelfth-century piers were re-

47

Twyford church from across the meadows

used. Constructed of flint with bands of brick, the new building, in a Perpendicular style, is scaled up to perhaps twice the size of a medieval equivalent, and at close quarters it can seem over-size. However, perhaps Waterhouse was prepared to accept this in exchange for a singularly impressive building which remains in a setting little changed since he constructed it. Even the mighty yew tree which still stands in the churchyard is perhaps as ancient as the re-used piers from the old church.

Once the home of Dr Shipley, Bishop of St Asaph and sympa-thizer with the American struggle for independence, Twyford House stands in the main street east of the church. It has an early eighteenth-century front, with three narrow first-floor windows at the centre above a later wide pedimented doorcase. The gate piers and ironwork at the entrance to the driveway, which appear to be of a similar date to the doorway, assist in creating a grand frontage within a relatively small space. In 1771 Benjamin Franklin was the bishop's guest and wrote part of his autobiography in the house. A portrait by Nollekins on a monument in the church commemorates Dr Shipley, who died in 1788.

Twyford School, almost opposite Twyford House but away from the main street, is one of the oldest preparatory schools in

Twyford House

49

the country and can claim to have had its origin in a Roman Catholic school founded in the 1690s at Silkstead, a hamlet a mile to the west. This school moved to Segar's Buildings in Twyford in 1696 and Alexander Pope spent a short time there when he was eight years old. His stay was short, it is recorded, because he lampooned his master. The establishment was flourishing in 1733 with 'upwards of one hundred scholars', but financial difficulties are thought to have followed, and with the outcry against Popery after the '45 Stuart rising the school closed. A gap in the history of the school then follows until 1793 when Segar's Buildings were sold, and let by a new owner to a Mr Hannington for 'a school for the sons of middle-class persons'. Part of the school may have later moved to the vicarage—was this the rectory east of the church? In 1809 it moved to the house forming part of the present school. Segar's Buildings were pulled down soon after the last war.

In 1815 the Rev. J. G. Bedford became headmaster and made additions to the buildings, including Upper School, where the headmaster sat at the northern end of the room, the Second Master at the southern end, and other masters at the sides. Mr Bedford's eyesight began to fail towards the end of his time at the school, but it is said that his daughter Mary assisted him to keep in touch with his pupils.

Thomas Hughes, author of *Tom Brown's Schooldays* published in 1857, was a pupil at the school and described methods of teaching and maintaining discipline in his book which might be based upon his experiences at Twyford. His remarks were derogatory, but not specifically aimed at Twyford: he wished to draw attention to the shortcomings of such schools in general. Tom Brown went on to Rugby but, in the old days at least, many Twyfordians went to Winchester College.

The house occupied by the school in 1809 remains, but it has had many additions. The old schoolroom including the head-master's desk has survived. A fine chapel was built in 1869 during the Headship of the Rev. Latham Wickham with the assistance of the Archbishop of Dublin, the Bishops of Ely, St Asaph and Winchester and others, including masters and parents. The response was greater than expected and a quite large, pleasantly Victorian chapel was built which remains in constant use with very few alterations. The grounds and playing-fields have been increased from time to time and are now extensive.

The railway embankment may be seen in the valley at Twyford, where it takes a rather straighter course than the river and

Twyford School from the playing-fields

follows the general direction of the Itchen Navigation cut by one of the earliest pioneers of canal construction, Godfrey de Lucy, Bishop of Winchester in the twelfth century. His Itchen Navigation linked New Alresford, Winchester and Southampton and was reported to be in service as late as 1662 when improvements were made. It is now derelict.

From the A335 Eastleigh road south of Twyford, a lane to Otterbourne crosses the valley past Brambridge House, a mansion of about 1870 built on the site of the family home of Mrs Fitzherbert, who married George IV. Near here, across the Itchen Navigation, was Otterbourne church which dated to the thirteenth century. Only a few gravestones in tangled undergrowth remain in this melancholy place, where past generations have erected memorial stones to perpetuate the remembrance of their dead, but the graveyard is desecrated. Apparently church authorities took the practical view and wasted neither time nor money on an unusable church, or on preserving the memory of the departed, responsibility for the abandoned cemetery resting with the Local Authority. The Redundant Churches Fund might have provided the only hope of saving it, and their work cannot be too highly commended, but I am told that the church had become too ruinous even for their help.

The lane continues across the valley to the old Chandler's Ford road and the village of Otterbourne, where Charlotte Yonge lived. A Victorian novelist and author of children's books, she was born in 1823 and lived at Otterbourne House until her later years when she moved to 'Elderfield', a house in the village main street. She taught at the village Sunday School for seventy-one years and edited a periodical called the *Monthly Packet*, aimed to advance Anglican ideals amongst young women. She died at Otterbourne in 1901 and is buried near the memorial to John Keble in the churchyard of St Matthew's Church, Otterbourne.

St Matthew's Church is on the old Chandler's Ford road opposite the lane from the ruined churchyard. Externally it is an uninviting building, made drab by the grey-blue bricks of which it is built. These are local bricks and can look well when contrasted with others of a good red colour.

Otterbourne in Charlotte Yonge's time came within the parish of Hursley, to which John Keble arrived as vicar in 1836, and the building of the church in 1837-9 by William Yonge, Charlotte's father, must have been inspired by the arrival in the parish of a well-known and controversial churchman. Owen Carter, who at that time was working on the admirable library in Jewry Street, Winchester, designed the church, and the site was given by Magdalen College, Oxford. Keble gave four hundred pounds towards the cost. Erected in two phases, the north aisle and apse were later additions. The interior is rich in detail and greatly enhanced by the roof—a forest of timber with cusped arches—and a large rood screen in the same flamboyant style erected to commemorate Charlotte Yonge. A balustrade across the chancel is said to be Flemish, purchased in London by William Yonge who also obtained the carved panels adapted for the pulpit by the addition of two duplicates in cast iron.

The influence of the Oxford Movement is unmistakably evident in the church furnishings, with crosses, roods, reserved sacrament, candles and so forth, although I was not aware of the incense which I fondly associate with going to church when a lad. It is possible to stand inside St Matthew's and imagine the amazement with which this interior would have been regarded by most churchgoers in 1839. It would have appeared to be a return to Popery with all the evil implied to a Protestant at that time. The Movement created the 'High', as opposed to the 'Low' Church within the Church of England

The lych-gate, Hursley church

and it is a division that still exists—if not in fact, then certainly in the minds of many churchmen.

The Movement started in Oxford—perhaps a sermon preached by John Keble before the university on 14 July, 1833, marked its beginning. The so-called Tracts followed, which spoke out against the alleged liberalizing and reforming movements in the church, as well as state control and the increasing interference by government in the Church's financial affairs.

There were inevitable losses to the Roman Catholic Church, notably John Henry Newman, but Keble was a steadying influence. He had a brilliant career at Oxford which he left when he came to the parish of Hursley at the age of forty-four, and served there until his death, not caring to seek, or accept, preferment.

Hursley is a little over two miles to the west of Otterbourne and was associated with Cromwell's son, Richard and also with Henry de Blois, Bishop of Winchester, who built a fortified palace near there called Merdon Castle. When the castle was abandoned a new house, the Great Lodge, was built and this became the home of Richard Cromwell and his family. Later,

53

when Great Lodge was taken down to make way for Hursley Park, it is said that the Great Seal of Commonwealth England was found concealed in a wall—but I cannot vouch for the truth of this. The Heathcote family bought Hursley from Cromwell's daughters and it was William Heathcote who persuaded John Keble to accept the living at Hursley in 1836.

Keble rebuilt the eighteenth-century church at Hursley between 1839 and 1866 with the help of the architect J.P. Harrison of Oxford, a follower of the Oxford Movement, using royalties from his 'Christian Year' and a second edition of his *Lyra Innocentium*. The exterior is not exceptional, but the fine original stained glass by William Wailes remains and the interior arrangement and fittings were designed according to High Church ideas.

The lych-gate, combining a small house which I am told was once occupied by the verger, is at the south-east corner of the churchyard and makes a very good composition. It is typical of its time, with more than a faint hint of Pugin's influence.

In 1902 Hursley Park was altered by George Cooper, who was a great benefactor to the village. He died in 1940, shortly after he had offered the house to Lord Beaverbrook for use during the war and Vickers-Armstrong moved in to work there on the Spitfire. The house is now in the hands of IBM.

Many buildings in Hursley are of interest. These include the Audit House, now a private residence, which was built as the Estate Office where rents were paid, various estate cottages, the old blacksmith's shop, the school and the schoolmasters' house. There is also a handsome row of continuous jettied houses at the southern end of the main street.

In the grounds of Cranbury Park to the north of Chandler's Ford are fragments from the north transept of Netley Abbey, reassembled about 1760 by Thomas Lee Dummer, or his son, as a folly to conceal the gamekeeper's house from the mansion. The red brick house is still there, built into the back of the 'ruin'. Previously the Winchester Butter Cross had been purchased as a folly, but its removal by Mr Dummer was prevented by irate citizens. A replica in plaster was made which disintegrated and was replaced with the Netley Abbey stones.

Chandler's Ford, part of the northern spread of Southampton, has claims to fame. It provided bricks for the London Law Courts from Mr Bull's brickworks, and legend tells how the charcoal burner William Purkess, who conveyed the body of Rufus from the New Forest to Winchester, passed through the village.

Eastleigh, south of Chandler's Ford, grew as a railway town around Bishopstoke Junction and the original station, by Sir William Tite, remains with additions. The Railway Hotel is another survivor. Development to the west of the railway occurred following the decisions to move the carriage works in

A row of continuous jettied houses, Hursley

1891 and then the locomotive workshops in 1903, from Nine Elms to Eastleigh.

The village of Bishopstoke has retained some character and is separated from Eastleigh by the Itchen. There are thatched cottages in Spring Lane, a plain stuccoed Manor House on an island between the channels of the river, the Georgian Old Rectory, and the exciting Itchen House of the mid-nineteenth century, with low gables and carved bargeboards.

North Stoneham stands on the last strip of countryside before the outskirts of Southampton begin. North Stoneham Park, the home of the Fleming family, most notably Lord Chief Justice Fleming, who died in 1613, was demolished many years ago and only a ruinous lodge near the church now remains. The church is unusual: it was rebuilt at the end of the sixteenth century in the Gothic style which had lingered on as a survival, not a revival. Old work has been incorporated, possibly from the previous church, with some from elsewhere. Opposite, the early nineteenth-century stock brick Old Rectory has a good doorcase and a large bow window.

Suburbia begins at Stoneham, which is at first wooded and pleasant, but housing density increases the nearer one gets towards the old walled town of Southampton.

4 Southampton

It was inevitable, with the increasing demands of the sea traffic serving the hinterlands of southern England, that the arrow-head shaped piece of land situated between the estuaries of the Test and the Itchen which converge at the head of Southampton Water, should provide the site for a seaport. The location is highly desirable on several counts. It is sheltered, almost land-locked, being about six miles up Southampton Water, nowhere much more than a mile wide, and protected to the south by the Isle of Wight. There is a deep-water channel and also the advantage of the tide, which only ebbs for three and three-quarter hours out of the twelve.

A port was established at what is now Bitterne on the eastern shore of the Itchen and flourished in the first and second centuries. Known to the Romans as Clausentum, it was linked to Roman Britain through the road system. It declined in the third century, but in the late fourth century, when military occupation of Portchester Castle ceased, it was defended by a stone wall and ditch as one of the 'Saxon Shore' forts, refortified by Count Theodosius to defend the coast against Saxon raids around 369.

Later, by the eighth century, the Saxons became established on the west bank of the Itchen at a place they called Hamwic, which was in the area around the present St Mary's Church and the technical college.

Further development occurred to the south-west, on the River Test. This may have been known as Hamtun, from which the name Hampshire is believed to be derived. On the shore near what is now Canute Road, legend records that King Canute demonstrated to flattering courtiers that he could not stop the incoming tide.

Soon after the Conquest a castle and earth fortifications were built by the Normans, who realized the value of Southampton as a port providing contact with France, a contact retained through the centuries and through two world wars to the present day. In wartime the port was an embarkation point for armies. The archers of Crécy and Agincourt embarked there, as did the armies of the two World Wars. Southampton was a member of the Staple and trade prospered, with the wool and cloth of medieval England a considerable export to the Mediterranean. In exchange ships from Genoa and Venice brought goods of all kinds from the East. Wine from France was also a major import. Southampton, conveniently placed for this trade, was nearer the French coast than London, and road links were reasonably good.

With a reduction of the wool trade the port declined in the Tudor period and the ascendancy of London was felt, with the result that throughout the seventeenth and eighteenth centuries the port catered mostly for regional trade. During the eighteenth century spa waters were found to the north of the town and development schemes in the early nineteenth century transformed it into a favoured resort. Stuccoed villas and terraces began to spring up near Queen's Park and a few buildings of this period remain, having survived the bombing of 1940, principally in Portland Street, Palmerston Road, and further north in the area of Carlton Crescent and Bedford Place.

Prosperity as a seaport returned when the railway linked the town with London in 1840 and new open docks were built—the Princess Alexandra Dock was opened in 1842. From this time a modern port began to expand. A high point was reached in the early decades of this century with the glamorous passenger trade of the White Star Line and the arrival of the Cunard 'Queens' which berthed at the Ocean Terminal on the east side of Ocean Dock, opened in 1911. The *Queen Mary* was in service by 1935.

Deep-water expansion took place at the mouth of the Test, and the Western Docks, completed in 1934, involved the reclamation of some four hundred acres and provided more than a mile of deep-water quay. The King George V Graving Dock, built in 1933, is situated in this area. In 1967 the Western Docks were extended for the container business and the railway still serves the berths at Millbrook, with modern facilities for containers. An overhead network of roads has been slung across the landscape to allow access for lorries, but the railway could be more efficient if its potential was sensibly exploited nationwide.

At the time of writing the docks handle less passenger traffic than formerly, and have a rival in Portsmouth. Poor labour relations may have been a cause, but more importantly, via Portsmouth is a shorter sea-route to France. Many changes, however, have taken place since the devastating destruction of the German bombing and the perhaps inevitable loss of the luxury passenger trade of the big 'liners' did much to change the character of Southampton.

The area of the old walled town is not large—only a quarter of a mile across, east to west, and half a mile long, north to south—so during the fierce aerial attacks and the destruction of 1940 it suffered terribly. Was it destroyed for ever? I feel there is no 'atmosphere' in the place now. The medieval buildings that survive remain as museums or museum pieces, beautifully and lovingly restored, labelled, documented, and preserved. Only perhaps in Bugle Street can I feel a little of the spirit of an ancient place. This is a personal observation—I would not wish to venture criticism, or suggest that the sterling work of the restorers should be denigrated. I also realize that new buildings have to replace old—it has always been so. A new Southampton is rising out of the dust, but there are times when one indulges in looking back.

The walls of the old town, which have survived to a considerable extent, date in part to the early thirteenth century. However, in 1338 a vicious Sunday morning attack by the French prompted further improved defence works. The principal defences had been placed on the landward side—now the shoreline had to be strengthened. By 1370 stone walls had been built to the west and south and much of this work remains. On what was once the western shore, where the sea lapped the quay, it can be seen how the frontages of existing houses—one at least is Norman—were built into them. These walls are some of the finest and most dramatic defences in England.

Wind Whistle Tower, known less romantically as Arundel Tower after Sir John Arundel, who might have added to this thirteenth-century tower when governor of the castle in the 1370s—stands on a natural cliff which once stood above the waters of the Test estuary, until land reclamation in 1850, and very picturesque it must have been.

The wall continues southward against the cliff, serving as a retaining wall, to Catchcold Tower, built in the fifteenth century. South of this stood Castle Bailey wall, with the site of the castle mound behind it. Further south an interruption in the continuity of the wall is caused by a modern development opposite the Central Swimming Baths. Like so many similar examples one sees there has been a sincere effort to harmonize

Arundel or Wind Whistle Tower, Southampton

new with old without resort to imitation of historic styles. However, the simplest mistakes seem to be made. Ghastly rubber-textured dull red bricks have been used and detail lacks relief—the string courses and dentils do not project enough to cast good shadows. Result: an unpleasant colour and surface, insipid details, and not a hope of escaping disastrous comparisons with adjacent medieval work.

Westgate, in the old Town Wall near the nineteenth-century stuccoed Royal Standard public house, provides access to the south-west corner of the old town. It is fourteenth century and although in itself perhaps not too impressive, it was the main

Westgate, Southampton

gate to the West Quay which in medieval times was at the water's edge. Through this gate passed the armies of Edward III in 1345 to fight at Crécy, and later Henry V and his longbowmen passed through bound for Harfleur and the victory at Agincourt. On the landward side of the gate a small square surrounded by a very good modern housing development takes its place with courtesy and due deference to the ancient gateway. Perhaps a romantic could dream a little in this square and imagine the crowded scenes as armies, foreign merchants, agents, and all the bustle of a busy seaport crowd through this gateway to the ships on the quay beyond.

The gate tower is bordered by brick Georgian houses to the north and a two-storey building to the south, built against the wall, which has a stone ground floor below a timber-framed structure with long curving braces. Documentary evidence records that originally it was a fish market with a guild hall above it, and that it stood in St Michael's Square in the 1420s. It was moved to its present site about 1600 and then served as a merchants' store. It is now a lecture hall but may be visited by special arrangement.

The fourteenth-century walls continue from Westgate to the south-west corner of Town Quay, where there is an arcaded section of five bays. Some are not original, and three northerly arcades were constructed in 1900. Visible evidence of the wall above ground ends at this point and does not appear again until further east at the Watergate opposite the entrance to the Town Quay at gate number six. This area is full of interest. There are two monuments: one, the Stella Memorial, commemorates a stewardess named Mary Ann Rogers who was lost after assisting to rescue passengers when a ship sank in 1899. It is a delicate octagonal structure with open rounded arches supporting the roof. The other monument reminds us that the *Mayflower* and the *Speedwell* put in at West Quay in 1620. The Pilgrim Fathers had sailed from Rotherhithe on the Thames and were to make an unplanned call at Plymouth before finally facing the Atlantic crossing.

At the corner of Bugle Street are two contrasting buildings. On the west side, the Victorian mansion of 1846 by T.S. Hack is an impressive Italianate classical design with a Tuscan colonnade across the ground storey front. There is a wide cornice, and the whole design has exceptionally fine detail for the period. The house was built for the Yacht Club. On the east side is the Wool House, a stone-built fourteenth-century warehouse, once the property of Beaulieu Abbey and a store for wool before shipment. The building was used as a store until its restoration and careful conversion as a Maritime Museum. The arched collar brace roof has survived almost unchanged since the fourteenth century.

Bugle Street contains more of interest: there are several eighteenth-century houses—in particular, on the west side there is a five-bay Georgian house with a pedimented Doric

The Duke of Wellington, Bugle Street, Southampton

doorcase—and opposite, the Duke of Wellington, a sixteenth-century timber-framed public house, has a jettied and gabled frontage. The house was damaged in the war and has been much restored. Georgian houses lead up to the flamboyant Tudor House built by Sir John Dawtrey, in a style more expected and acceptable in a Cheshire landscape. Built in the early sixteenth century and incorporating an older hall it went through a period of some ill treatment, but was restored and given to the town as a museum. In the garden at the rear is access to a twelfth-century Norman house, the frontage of which was built into the western defence walls. Two arches leading to the quay have been blocked, but are pierced by two gunports of the fourteenth century, which are possibly the earliest in Britain.

Tudor House faces St Michael's Church, the oldest and most venerated of Southampton's churches, mercifully spared destruction during the war. Its origins are Norman: it was cruciform in plan and the base of the central Norman tower remains with its arches; the upper part may have been rebuilt, but the bell-stage dates to the late nineteenth century when the eighteenth-century stone spire—which had replaced a medieval one—was rebuilt and heightened. The plan of the church is now rectangular, with chancel and chapels and a nave with aisles. The interior was much altered in the early nineteenth century by Francis Goodwin, who replaced the nave arcades and put in galleries which were removed in the 1870s. The church contains a medieval lectern from the blitzed Holy Rood Church and one of Hampshire's four Tournai marble fonts.

Eastwards along Town Quay is a nineteenth-century brick warehouse, derelict at the time of writing, but well worth preserving. Next comes a nineteenth-century Italianate façade which makes an interesting contrast to the adjacent fourteenth-century Watergate on the corner of High Street. Sections of this southern gateway to the town survived in part of a house which was damaged in the bombing and the tower has been cleared of debris and repaired. West of the tower is the so-called King Canute's Palace. It was a first-floor hall house, part of the original walls surviving and revealing interesting detail which dates the house from the twelfth century—not Canute's time. These walls will be preserved along with the Water Tower and other excavated medieval vaults nearby to be contained within a small park terminated at the west end by the Wool House.

Eastwards across High Street and down Winkle Street is the Hospital of St Julian, founded in the late twelfth century as an

Tudor House Museum, Bugle Street, Southampton

almshouse for travellers. The houses around the little church were rebuilt in 1861. The church, of 1190, used by French-speaking Protestants from the sixteenth century until 1939, was restored in 1861.

The God's House Gate, also known as Saltmarsh Gate and built in the thirteenth century, stands at the end of Winkle Street. Lambcote Tower, the building above the gate, served as a prison. The larger God's House Tower, built in the fifteenth century and now a museum, combines with the Gate to form an

65

impressive front to the Town Quay. This is an interesting area of the walled town, as northwards from here may be seen one of the earliest surviving sections of the wall. The medieval East Ditch ran along this side of the wall and was made part of a canal built in 1795. This linked the ditch with the Andover Canal at Redbridge near Totton, and thence to Romsey and the Test to Fullerton, the Anton Valley and Andover. Unfortunately the Southampton project failed, but the ditch remained until the 1850s.

To the east is Queen's Park, which was developed as a seaside resort in the 1830s, and in Queen's Terrace, Latimer Street and Oxford Street, there are stuccoed houses of the period. The beach followed the line of the present Canute Road but when development of the open beach took place an area of leisure by the sea turned to big business with ocean-going ships. A railway terminus constructed in 1840 heralded changes to come, but did not immediately affect the quality or desirability of the area. Property appeared in Bernard Street nearby in 1840, and also in Queen's Terrace. The coming of the railway seems to have been of assistance in the promotion of the spa, as it greatly reduced the amount of goods and passenger traffic passing by road through the town and congesting the streets.

At the corner of Terminus Terrace and Canute Road BBC Southern Television and Radio Solent is housed in what was once the South Western Hotel, opened in 1872 to serve an expanding passenger trade.

Terminus Terrace leads northward to Marsh Lane, St Mary's Street and St Mary's Church. This was the church of Hamwic, and was looked upon as the mother church of Southampton. Nothing remains of the medieval building, indeed nothing remains of a series of successors to it: even the church, built by G.E. Street in the late 1870s, was bombed. Rebuilt in the 1950s, there is little of Street's original design, except the tower and spire built from his designs in 1914 which fortunately survived the bombing and are undoubtedly superb. It can be seen to good effect across Hoglands, one of the many open spaces which grace the city centre and recall an earlier period when these common lands were farmed. Hoglands was arable land divided into strips and farmed in common.

Hoglands and Houndwell Park together extend westward from St Mary's towards Bargate and the pedestrian area of Above Bar. Palmerston Road divides the two parks and ends at a traffic roundabout to the south near some of the city's large stores. This traffic island is graced by a cast-iron gas standard,

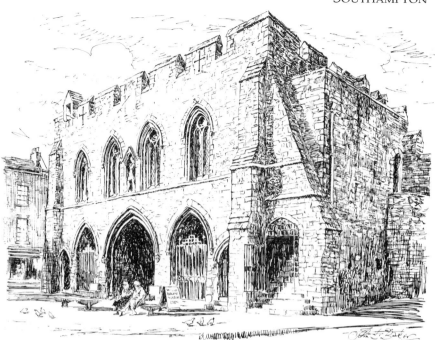

Bargate, Southampton

which, if not elegant in design, is amusing. It was erected as 'a tribute of respect and gratitude to William Chamberlayne Esquire for his magnificent gift of the iron columns supporting the public lights of this Town MDCCCXXII'.

In this area are more sections of the town wall, marking its northern perimeter and originally joining nearby Bargate, the northern gate of Southampton. When electric trams were introduced the suggestion that Bargate should be demolished was seriously considered, but it survived, and the trams were routed through its centre arch by lowering the roadway to provide headroom. The open-topped trams had ample room, but they were later replaced by specially designed lower, covered-top double-deckers. However, in the 1930s the adjoining walls, and the houses built around them, were demolished so that traffic went around, not through, the arch. The dignity of Bargate as the principal gateway is now lost. At best it looks like a triumphal arch, but is more like a stranded leviathan. It is a pity that the pedestrian area of Above Bar could not have been brought down to the gate and the gyrating traffic kept away.

The only original work remaining in the gate is the twelfth-century round-headed central arch—the rest has been rebuilt over the centuries. In the late thirteenth century the towers on the north side were built, as well as those on the south façade. The pointed arches to the north and south of the main opening are fourteenth century. A century later the north front was made imposing by the addition of a central feature, canted forward between the thirteenth-century towers, and capped with a bold machicolated parapet. This has been attributed to Wynford or Yevele, both royal master-builders. Above the gateway was the early Guildhall, now a museum. Much restoration work has been done on Bargate, particularly on the southern façade where a statue of Queen Anne, now in the Guildhall, was replaced by the statue of George III dressed up as a Roman. The roof of the Guildhall is unfortunately not original but a nineteenth-century replacement.

Above Bar is a modern pedestrian shopping-precinct—the introduction of pedestrian areas is popular with modern planners and is a commendable way of keeping the dreaded motor car out of city centres. The architecture here is dull, unless one side-steps into Portland Street which recalls the late eighteenth and early nineteenth centuries when Southampton aspired to be a spa. In Portland Place the Victoria Rooms had the Victoria Spa 'situated in the grounds' where 'the finest chalybeate waters in the kingdom' could be taken. The view across the sea from the grounds was highly commended. Indeed, below on the western shore Frederick Prince of Wales had bathed in 1750, and in a publication of 1850 we are informed that 'the bathing-machines are in a good situation at West Quay'. In the High Street is the Dolphin Hotel, a late eighteenth-century red brick building with the great bow windows which were popular at this time. Behind the hotel a beautiful room is to be found: this was once the Assembly Room, around which the genteel society of fashionable Southampton revolved. It colours our thoughts of this period in Southampton if we recall that Jane Austen and her mother lived in Castle Street from 1805-9 and may have attended functions in this room.

Above Bar ends near the Civic Centre which includes the Law Courts, Guildhall, Municipal Offices, the Art Gallery and Library and was built in the 1930s by E. Berry Webber. Surprisingly it has not dated: it owes a little to the classic tradition and is planned as four blocks forming a quadrangle, the outer façade of each block designed as a symmetrical composition. The whole composition benefits from the tall clocktower set to the west above the Law Courts.

The Cenotaph by Lutyens should be seen—it is in the park north of the Civic Centre. Another memorial, in East Park near the corner of Above Bar Street and Brunswick Place, is to the engineer-officers lost in the *Titanic*, which sailed from Southampton on her fated maiden voyage.

There is more stucco of the 1820s in Carlton Crescent, and in Bedford Place, number seventy-four and its neighbours are particularly attractive. In Carlton Place a row of four houses with bow windows is typical of the Southampton style and

Carlton Place, Southampton

69

Bedford Place, Southampton

some of the best in the area. There was an indoor riding school in Carlton Place, claimed to be 'the finest building in the Kingdom devoted to this purpose, being lofty and extensive'. Equestrian displays were presented there.

5 The New Forest

The toll-bridge at Eling, where the Bartley stream runs into the Test estuary, is the last of its kind in Hampshire and still provides the shortest route from Southampton to the western shore of Southampton Water. On the causeway there is a tide mill, now a working museum and very popular with visitors. Both the mill and the toll-bridge were owned by Winchester College until 1939 when their interests in the mill and the bridge were given to the New Forest District Council.

Eling church stands above the estuary and the sloping ground to the mud flats below is said to have inspired the words of Isaac Watts' hymn, 'There is a land of pure delight . . . Sweet fields beyond the swelling floods.'

Marchwood is a large modern power-station, but the village of Marchwood has a rural setting and is, after all, on the edge of the New Forest. Dibden also has a similar air about it and Hythe nearby, a small town with a Georgian high street, has a pier with an electric railway built in 1879, which extends seven hundred yards across the mud flats to serve the ferry from Southampton. The Drummond Arms, a substantial mid-nineteenth-century building which took its name from the Drummond family of Cadland House, adds character to the waterfront.

The presence of the great one-thousand acre Esso Fawley refinery has not had the expected devastating effect on the rural character of Fawley village or the surrounding country: in fact wildlife has prospered in the area. Fawley church, opposite the main gate to the refinery, has a charming country setting unspoilt by the discreet refinery office building nearby. Damaged during the war it was restored in 1954 by Randoll Blacking and contains twelfth-century and late thirteenth-century work—the Norman west door is particularly fine. Now reset in the wall beneath the east window, a small round-headed opening cut from a single stone could be from an earlier Saxon church on the site.

Eling Tide Mill

Below the village at Ashlett Creek, a small harbour used by leisure craft, there is a tide mill dated 1818. Now no longer working, it is also a clubhouse for Esso refinery workers.

In the late 1920s Calshot was associated with the RAF High Speed Flight and the series of Schneider Trophy Races, all won by the RAF who retained the trophy. Princess Flying Boats operated commercial flights from here and during the Second World War Coastal Command used the base for training aircrews using Sunderland flying-boats. Calshot, now owned by the Hampshire County Council, is a large Recreation Centre. The complex is on Calshot Spit which curves, hook-like, across Southampton Water to terminate at the north-east with Calshot Castle, built by Henry VIII, who was concerned by the possibility of aggressive action by Francis I of France. The stone for it is said to have been brought from the monastic buildings of Netley and Beaulieu almost within months of their surrender.

Eaglehurst, a mid-eighteenth-century mansion built by

Temple Simon Luttrell, is not open to the public and remains secluded, but Luttrell's Tower can be seen from the shingle beach. It stands near the edge of rising ground with steps down to the shore—a castellated folly both delightful and ingenious, with Gothic windows and stair turret. Marconi put the place to practical use during his experiments with wireless telegraphy. Queen Victoria visited Eaglehurst with the intention of having the mansion as a country retreat, but she eventually chose a site on the Isle of Wight.

The coast here is pleasant. Woods come down to the shore in many places, and at Lepe, where the Hampshire County Council has created a Country Park, the road winds past a row of coastguard cottages and a shingle beach to skirt the shore of Beaulieu River, and on to Exbury where the gardens, which are famous for their rhododendrons, are open to the public. Exbury village is dominated by a grand watertower made of brick which stores mains water for supplying the village and the

73

gardens. Less conspicuous is an excellent little church built in 1907 in a late Gothic style, which stands nearby.

The road from Exbury meets the B3054 which runs south-westward to Beaulieu, where a Cistercian abbey was founded by King John in 1204. The Cistercians were farmers, hence the fine series of barns built in the granges of their abbeys. They preferred a remote valley site for their monasteries and Beaulieu in Norman French meant a 'beautiful place' in the sense that it could be turned to good agricultural use by the labour of the monks. The site of the abbey is on moor and heath at the edge of

A Cistercian monk

the New Forest and is served by the Beaulieu River. It is bounded to the south by several miles of Solent shore which provided saltings and fishing. Access to it by water was a great assistance in the beginning as building materials could be brought by boat. Freestone for facing the exterior came from Binstead on the Isle of Wight, stone for the interior was from Caen, Purbeck provided the marble and roofing slate came from Cornwall. Floor tiles may have been made from a local clay. Building work progressed rapidly: the church was in use by 1227 and completed by 1247. Advanced for its time, with a plan of French design, it had an ambulatory and radiating chapels around an apsidal east end.

Beaulieu Abbey surrendered in April 1538 and was granted to Thomas Wriothesley. Stone was robbed for the building of

Calshot Castle and Hurst Castle in 1539, but the fourteenth-century inner gatehouse was retained to form the nucleus of a house—Palace House. Work on this took place at intervals—the second Duke of Montagu is thought to have built the round towers in 1722 as fortification against a feared French attack. Then in 1872 Sir Arthur Blomfield was commissioned to do work there.

The plan of the church and the monastic building is traced on the ground and a few walls and arches remain standing. Part of the west range also stands—including a vaulted undercroft—and a section now adapted for use as a restaurant.

The Tide Mill, Beaulieu, with the Abbey Gate in the background

Fortunately the abbey refectory, the frater, survived to become the parish church—hence a church with a north-south axis. This has been described as a 'noble room', which indeed it is. It has a reader's pulpit with a stair contained within the east wall behind an open arcade of Purbeck marble shafts set in pairs. The pulpit is not original, but the bracket supporting it is thirteenth century and beautifully carved with sprays of leaves. Beaulieu Abbey and grounds are open to the public and contain the Beaulieu National Motor Museum and other attractions.

The abbey had outlying chapels and granges and sheep farming was a considerable source of income. At St Leonards,

an important grange a mile south of Bucklers Hard, is a ruined chapel of about 1300. There are also important remains of a large barn, now roofless, although the east and part of the west stone gables remain. Traces of evidence give an indication of the form of its roof construction, for which a reconstruction has been suggested by Professor Walter Horn and Professor C. Born with reference to the Beaulieu barn at Great Coxwell near Oxford and others of the Order in France.

The lanes from St Leonards lead to Bucklers Hard, planned in the early eighteenth century by the second Duke of Montagu as a quay for trade with the West Indies. His scheme failed because the French took over the islands of St Vincent and St Lucia—of which he had been made Governor before his ships and a hundred settlers arrived, but the port of 'Montagu Town' which he had planned on the Beaulieu River survived the set-back.

The Duke died in 1749 but the small hamlet named Bucklers Hard continued to trade by handling timber until it turned to shipbuilding, or to be more precise, until it became increasingly well known for its ships. In 1698 the *Salisbury* had been built for

Bucklers Hard, New Forest

the Navy at, or near, Bucklers Hard. During the mid and later eighteenth century many ships for the Navy were built there. The most famous was the *Agamemnon*, launched in 1781, Nelson's first command and his favourite ship. The master-builder Henry Adams, who came in 1749 and lived in the house—now a hotel called the Master-Builder—undoubtedly contributed to the success of the yard.

Bucklers Hard still engages in the building of small ships and provides facilities for yachtsmen and pleasure-boats passing up and down the river. It is also popular with land-based visitors to the late eighteenth century cottages that line the wide street ending in a superb view across the river. Apart from the Master-Builder, the village public house and hotel, there is a maritime museum and in one of the cottages a small chapel.

Lymington, an important sailing centre on the Solent shore, was probably a Saxon port and shipbuilding took place there in Norman times continuing until the eighteenth century. From the twelfth century the town's wealth was derived from the production of salt from seawater, until the introduction of rock salt killed the trade in the nineteenth century. Celia Fiennes, that indomitable traveller, witnessed the process of gaining salt by evaporating seawater and reported it fully. A boiling house and many of the old saltings can be identified at Woodside and are evidence of the once considerable extent of the trade.

Quay Hill and High Street are the most memorable streets in the town and include some handsome Georgian houses. The church stands at the top of High Street, and the unusual combination of an eighteenth-century cupola on a Gothic tower—albeit seventeenth-century Gothic—adds character. Nearby

Lymington

are gas lamps on Doric columns, some of the town's first lamps, set up by Admiral Sir H. Burrard Neal in 1832.

Westwards along the Solent shore, on a spit of land curving out to the narrow channel between the mainland and the Isle of Wight, is Hurst Castle. It was one of the defences built by Henry VIII, which, with Yarmouth Castle on the Isle of Wight opposite, provided defence for the western entrance to the Solent. Here Charles I was held in great discomfort for a little over two weeks in the December before his 'trial' and execution. The castle, which is open to the public during the summer months, can be reached along the strand. Directions to it are well signposted in the area, but parking space is limited.

A little to the north of Milford is Hordle where, in the church-yard, are the graves of twelve 'New Forest Shakers'. Led by Mrs Mary Ann Girling, the Shakers were a religious sect who danced and shook as they worshipped and who were established at Hordle by a wealthy patron. Local opinion became hostile and the sect, numbering over a hundred, mostly women and child-ren, was evicted. After great hardship they resettled and survived until the death of Mrs Girling in 1886.

From New Milton the B3055 regretfully turns at the realigned Hampshire-Dorset border away from Christchurch , which bureaucratically is not in Hampshire but historically always has been, and thus to many it will remain. The magnificent priory can be seen from the outskirts of the town, but our way must lead back into the New Forest.

Boldre church still has a rural setting although development is taking place around it. In 1777 William Gilpin arrived as the new vicar and was appalled by the dishonesty of the villagers who excelled at poaching and smuggling. During a long curacy—he remained until he died in 1804—he ran a village school with funds earned from his writing. His books assisted to formulate ideas concerning a 'natural' rendering of picturesque landscape as opposed to the stiff idealized 'Classical' inter-pretation associated with artists such as Claude. Illustrated with his own drawings—some of them etched by his brother Sawrey Gilpin, the horse painter—a series of volumes had an influence on the young Turner, whose extraordinary genius later became identified with a revolutionary approach to landscape painting. Southey, the Poet Laureate, was a friend of Gilpin, who married the poet and Caroline Bowers at Boldre following their long engagement.

Brockenhurst, to the north, began to expand after the arrival in 1847 of Castleman's Corkscrew—a railway from Southampton to Dorchester which crossed the New Forest and was 'axed' by Dr Beeching. The church is perhaps the earliest in the forest, with a Norman nave and a brick tower built in 1761. In the churchyard there is a large and ancient yew tree, and the grave of 'Brusher' Mills the adder-catcher, who either sold his catch alive or rendered it down for the fat.

Lyndhurst has been called the 'capital' of the New Forest and here the Verderers Court is held in the Kings House west of the church. The people of the forest jealously guard their 'ancient and ornamental woodlands', the management of which remains in their control through this court. There are ten Verderers, of whom five are officially appointed and five elected, and the Agisters are the 'police' of the Forest. Several thousand properties or 'hearths' have 'rights of common'—the rights are not vested in people—but only a relative few are taken up. However, large tracts of the forest are under the control of the Forestry Commission who administer the woodland on a commercial basis as specified by Acts of Parliament.

There is certainly no other place like the New Forest—it has the distinction of once being the preserve of English kings, and was jealously administered by them as a royal hunting-ground. It still has a 'managed' park-like 'wildness' and is nowhere utterly remote. William the Conqueror created it, imposing the

Lyndhurst, New Forest

extremely harsh Forest Law and he may have obliterated a number of hamlets in the process.

The church of St Michael Lyndhurst replaced a chapel of ease within the parish of Minstead when it was built in the 1860s. It is a large church in bright red and yellow brick and the nave roof is supported by carved wood angels, but perhaps the most notable features are the reredos by Lord Leighton, painted in 1864, in which he has depicted the Wise and Foolish Virgins, and the William Morris stained glass—the east window was designed by Burne-Jones. The grave of Alice Liddell—Lewis Carroll's 'Alice in Wonderland' is in the churchyard. She lived in a house called Cuffnells, demolished in the early 1950s, with her cricketer husband Reginald Hargreaves.

The parish church of Minstead, three miles to the north-west on rising ground above the village green, has additions dating from the seventeenth and eighteenth centuries which give the exterior an attractive 'domestic' appearance. The interior has west galleries and box pews—one with a fireplace—a three-decker pulpit of pale bleached oak, and the font, which is unusually placed in front of the pulpit, is late Norman work with carving on its four sides. The south transept provides the greatest seating accommodation, and the nave has a large eighteenth-century gallery with a modern gallery above it, said, on good authority, to have been put in to accommodate the gypsies. There is a delightful row of 'chapel' hat-pegs in the nave. In the churchyard is the grave of Sir Arthur Conan Doyle and his wife who lived in the village for a time.

Minstead is very much a village of the forest. It has a small green and a public house called the Trusty Servant, with a sign displaying the composite figure of a servant possessing all the physical modifications required to make him just that. Legend tells us, with its usual lack of reliable evidence, that William Rufus was warned of impending doom while at the village: he disregarded the warning and met his death at a spot near the A31, marked by the Rufus Stone.

Ringwood, on the western boundary of the county, is still a pleasant market town, where a nineteenth-century church replaces an earlier one which was entirely pulled down. A large eighteenth-century brick house in Christchurch Road is particularly fine and has giant order pilasters and a pediment.

Dame Alicia Lisle of Moyles Court near Ellingham, a village north of Ringwood, was a supporter of Cromwell. She was present at the execution of Charles I and is recorded to have said that her 'blood leapt in her veins to see the tyrant fall'. As an old lady of seventy she sheltered three fugitives of Monmouth's defeated army. For this she was brought before Judge Jeffreys at Winchester, who bludgeoned the jury to find her guilty and ordered her execution by fire. The sentence was mercifully changed to beheading. Moyles Court where she lived is now a school. It is built of brick laid in English bond, with a wide eaves cornice and hipped roof, and is a fine house, typical of many built in the second half of the seventeenth and early eighteenth centuries.

A mile away St Mary's Church, Ellingham, is thirteenth century, with a west end rebuilt of brick dated 1747; a porch also of brick, is a little earlier—1720. A fine interior is full of interest. The nave and chancel are both ceiled with barrel vaults of wood and the eastern end of the nave, with a tympanum above a fifteenth-century screen bearing texts, conceals a passage—once a rood loft gained from an opening in the chancel. A seventeenth-century family pew enclosed with screens stands in the nave, and there is also a pulpit of similar date with a preacher's hour-glass on the screen nearby. A reredos now at the west end of the nave, understandably attributed to Grinling Gibbons—I believe without proof—has pilasters, a dove and other carvings framing a painting. In the churchyard near the south wall of the nave stands the grave of Alicia Lisle, and also that of her daughter.

At Ibsley a delightful church of red brick built by a Salisbury architect named John Peniston in 1832 is the kind of building often ignored by architectural pundits. The nave and chancel are beneath one roof with a small tower or belfry at the west end. Lancet windows have small diamond and hexagonal panes typical of the period. Inside there is a monument to Sir John Constable and his wife, with the heads of their five children supported amongst the fruit of a vine, dated 1627 and from a previous church. Nearby Ibsley Bridge, which carries a lane to Harbridge over the Avon, is a handsome eighteenth-century structure of ashlar skilfully designed with a central elliptical arch flanked on each side by a segmental arch. From the bridge a view across the meadows is enhanced by Harbridge church. Rebuilt in 1838, the tower contains old stonework and the tracery in the windows in the nave and chancel is of artificial stone. The Countess of Normanton monument of 1841 in the nave is of the same material—possibly Coade Stone.

The Avon is met again at Fordingbridge, where it is spanned by a medieval bridge of seven arches, widened in 1841 without changing its style. Near the bridge in a corner of the recreation

ground is the bronze figure of Augustus John who was a powerful and often disruptive influence on British art almost until he
died aged eighty-three in 1961. His later years were spent at
Fryern Court, Upper Burgate, near Rockbourne.

The statue of Augustus John at Fordingbridge

In the eighteenth century the town suffered a disastrous fire
and therefore nearly all its architecture is nineteenth century—
the Town Hall is 1877. The church of St Mary, away from the
centre, is principally thirteenth century with a fifteenth-
century tower and north and south aisles. The north chapel is
early fifteenth century and was non-parochial, belonging to the
Templars and Hospitallers and finally passing to the Hospital of
St Cross at Winchester which still retains rights over it. This
may explain the high quality of the chapel and its fine hammer-
beam roof.

A worthwhile detour outside the forest boundary can be
made into a spur of Hampshire north-west of Fordingbridge,
which contains several very attractive villages and is rich in
earthworks dating from the Iron Age and others from a later
time. The great pioneer of modern scientific archaeology,
General Pitt-Rivers of Rushmore House in Wiltshire, worked
extensively in the district and two of his many excavations were

a Romano-British settlement at Woodcuttes and Bokerley Dyke at Woodyates, both on the Wiltshire border. The Bokerley Dyke crosses Martin Down in a north-westerly direction and is cut by the modern Blandford Forum road and the line of a Roman road, at what the general named Bokerley Junction. By a detailed and extensive excavation the general was able to prove conclusively that Bokerley Dyke was constructed in two periods. An earlier, lower embankment was crossed by the Roman road, but the much larger earthwork was constructed later than the Roman road as it extended across it. The date of the dyke was determined by Pitt-Rivers to be around AD 400, or even after the Roman Legions had left Britain. It was a defensive work on the boundary of the territory of the Durotriges, probably against attack from Saxon invaders.

In the vicinity two other earthworks, Grimms Ditch and Soldier's Ring should be seen, the latter thought to be a Roman cattle enclosure. Grimm is a synonym for Devil and occurs in the naming of similar earthworks in other parts of Britain. Unlike Bokerley Dyke, Grimms Ditch was not defensive but a boundary earthwork, probably surrounding lands in the possession of a Bronze Age overlord.

Damerham is four miles from Fordingbridge and has a small church beautifully sited on rising ground above the Allen River. It has been much altered but contains exceptionally fine twelfth- and thirteenth-century work and the tower is twelfth and thirteenth-century in its lower parts but left unfinished. The timber upper section is probably seventeenth century. Court Farm near the church has a Georgian front and some medieval detail—three arches and windows. There is also a large barn.

Rockbourne to the north of Damerham is said to be one of the prettiest villages in Hampshire. The wide, gently winding street runs alongside a winterbourne, Sweatfords Water, and is bordered by many thatched cottages, of which several, including Cruck Cottage, Glebe Cottage and Pennys Cottage, are of cruck construction.

The path to the church from the main street passes the vicarage, a plain Georgian house, and leads to the Manor House and the church. The Manor House has a thirteenth-century chapel and small fourteenth-century house to which is attached an Elizabethan east wing. There is also a large stone-built fifteenth-century barn with two waggon porches. The manor of Rockbourne was held by the Coopers in the seventeenth century and Ashley-Cooper was created Earl of Shaftesbury in 1672. Charles II told him that he was the 'wickedest' fellow in his dominions,

Rockbourne church

Rose Cottage, Martin

to which the Earl agreed that he probably was.

Rockbourne church is an early Norman building much changed in the thirteenth century and restored in the late nineteenth century by C.F. Ponting when an ornate porch was added. The bell turret is dated 1613.

The site of a large Roman villa was discovered south of the village by a farmer during ferreting. A.T. Morley-Hewitt, the owner, an amateur archaeologist and Fordingbridge estate agent identified and excavated most of it. The site was later acquired by the Hampshire County Council and is open to the public. West Park nearby was the home of the Coote family, and in 1828 the widow of General Sir Eyre Coote, who had commanded British troops in India, erected a one hundred foot monument to his memory. The Coote menfolk, it is said, were all bald: to be 'as bald as a coote' refers not to the water bird but to the Cootes!

Martin is the furthest west of this group of villages and its long street is lined with cottages, some of cob, many timber-framed

with brick infilling. Most are thatched, some have slate roofs. The Manor House forms the architectural nucleus or focal point, of the village street, and was reported by Aubrey, in the mid-seventeenth century, to have a small chapel with a tiled floor and to have belonged to the Earl of Shaftesbury. The chapel has gone, but tiles have been found.

When I called at Martin church, sheep were grazing the churchyard. This is a good old practice that is being used more frequently—more efficient than any motor mower—and here, very appropriately, Shepherd Lawes, the Isaac Balcombe of W.H. Hudson's *A Shepherd's Life* is buried.

Near the Wiltshire border, on Breamore Down, a fascinating earthwork is to be found. It is a mizmaze, not so ancient as Grimms Ditch—which turns up again about three-quarters of a mile away—but believed to have a mystical Christian origin. Unlike the Tudor Maze one was not expected to get lost in it, but to make steady progress along the twists of the turf path, praying as one approached the calvary at the centre. It symbolized the devious progress of a sinful life towards Paradise. The mizmaze is the only remaining feature of the priory at Breamore which was completely destroyed soon after the Dissolution in 1536.

Breamore House, an Elizabethan building damaged by fire in 1856, retains the front façade and inside, two particularly good fireplaces and a staircase. The house, and a transport museum housed in the eighteenth-century stables, are open to the public during the summer months.

The Saxon church of Breamore is one of the most exciting buildings in the county. The plan is cruciform, but not fully developed as in Norman or Gothic churches in which the transepts, nave and chancel are of equal width, with a tower placed over the crossing. The nave and chancel—the present chancel is not the original—were the same width as the tower, but the 'transepts'—*portici*—of which only the southern remains, were both narrower than the tower. Exciting features are to be seen but none surpass the inscription cut around the internal arch of the south *porticus*. The use of certain letters gives scholars the clue to its date of about AD 1000. Translated it reads 'Here the covenant is made manifest to thee'. Above the south doorway,

Breamore church

Brook, New Forest

within a Norman porch, is a large rood carved in stone. Regrettably, like a similar one at Headbourne Worthy, it has been mutilated and little more than the outlines of the figures can be seen. This sculpture was almost certainly destroyed soon after the 1547 decree in the name of Edward VI which ordered the

89

removal, or obliteration, of all images. The destruction that followed is too painful to contemplate. However, at Breamore we still have much of the original fabric of the church in which the fine Saxon sense of proportion is to be seen. The south *porticus* may be classed with the very finest architecture—it has an elusive element of perfection not to be found again in Britain until the thirteenth century.

At Upper Street, south of the church, is a picturesque group of timber-framed cottages of the sixteenth century and between the church and the main road from Fordingbridge is a low-lying expanse of common bordered by charming early Victorian almshouses where gaggles of geese graze contentedly.

Breamore Mill on the Avon ceased working in 1970. A turbine replaced the traditional waterwheel about 1900, but the growth of mass production methods in larger mills, and the loss of the railway in 1964, deprived the mill of work.

In 1717 Thomas Archer remodelled the church at Hale. He added the transepts and made the church cruciform in plan. The detail of door and window openings, and particularly the pilasters on the transepts, is all very typical of Archer.

The fine prospects of the Avon valley from the vantage points of Hale Park and the church are left behind for the wilder country of the forest as the road follows the Wiltshire boundary past Looshanger Copse and Hope Cottage towards Cadnam. The woods around Bramshaw are said to have provided the timber for the original roofs of Salisbury Cathedral and at Brook, a tiny village with thatched cottages, just before the tangle of roads at the Cadnam junction, it is not difficult to imagine that in the Green Dragon Dr. O.G.S. Crawford, the archaeologist and pioneer of air photography, overheard two local country-men speaking with all the intonations of the ancient Saxon tongue.

90

6 Romsey

The New Forest extends north of Brook to the A36 at Plaitford but sand and clay of the Hampshire Basin a little to the north of Romsey continues to influence the landscape, and wooded lanes lead to hamlets and farms which seem to be remote from main roads. Further south the M27 cuts a swathe across the landscape from Cadnam to Southampton and beyond, but even here, between feed roads and the areas of urban spread from Southampton, isolated pockets of rural calm survive untroubled by that other world on the trunk roads, the motorway and the housing developments.

East Wellow is such a place; there is no village, just a few scattered farms and cottages above the valley of the River Blackwater, a tributary of the Test. Florence Nightingale was born in Florence but spent her youth between Lea Hurst in Derbyshire and Embley Park, West Wellow a nineteenth-century Elizabethan-style brick house added to after 1895 and now a school. After a busy life she lived in London where she died in 1910 at the age of ninety. Her grave is in East Wellow churchyard.

St Margaret's Church, East Wellow is mostly thirteenth century, and the chancel, slightly later than the nave, has a beautiful east window of three grouped lancets with detached shafts. This flanks a medieval wall-painting, mostly contemporary with the first build, which depicts a St Christopher, the murder of Becket, and other subjects, together with sections of a repeat pattern composed of small rosettes covering sections of the nave and chancel walls. From the churchyard on the north side of the church there are views into Wiltshire. Amongst the trees by the A27 is the spire of St Leonard's Church at Sherfield English, built in 1902 for Lady Ashburton, a member of the Baring family, by Fred Bath of Salisbury, as a memorial to her daughter. It is an extravagance in brick and stone, the tower and spire have flying buttresses and pinnacles, and the interior

Florence Nightingale's grave, East Wellow

is rich in detail with Art Nouveau glass in the windows. From West Wellow the approach to Romsey should be northward along the lanes to the A27, from which, a little before its junction with the A31, there is a wide view of Romsey, the surrounding country, and the abbey across the River Test.

A religious house was established at Romsey in 907 by Edward the Elder for his daughter Ethelflaeda, eldest granddaughter of Alfred the Great, who is believed to be buried there. Under the influence of St Dunstan and Ethelwold, Bishop of Winchester, the foundation was reconstituted under Benedictine rule by King Edgar in 967. Ethelflaeda, a kinswoman of Edgar's wife, entered the abbey under the Abbess Morwenna. She later became abbess herself and was canonized, her name becoming linked with that of St Mary in the dedication of the abbey.

Romsey suffered a fierce Danish attack about 1002, and the nuns are believed to have taken refuge at Winchester. The extent of the damage to the abbey is unknown—the remains of an apse beneath the crossing is all that remains of this period.

Christine, sister of Edgar the Atheling and Margaret, Queen

of Scotland, took the veil at Romsey in 1086 and became abbess. Because of her presence the two daughters of Malcolm Canmore and Margaret, King and Queen of Scotland, were sent to the abbey to be educated. One of them, Matilda, married Henry I of England.

Mary, the daughter of King Stephen, became abbess in 1160 and it is just possible that her uncle, Henry de Blois, was involved in the building of the eastern half of the abbey.

From a place of esteem and wealth the abbey declined towards the end of the thirteenth century and discipline became lax. In 1283 a visitation was made by Bishop Peckham and it appears that he was critical of the irregularities he found. Rumour, understandably was rife, perhaps without real cause, at least until 1494. In that year the abbey was visited by order of Archbishop Morton, and the abbess, Elizabeth Brooke, was found to be guilty of perjury and adultery. The abbey was again visited in 1502 when there was a scandal involving the abbess Elizabeth Brooke and a Master Bryce. This forced the resignation of the abbess, and Joyce Rowse was elected in her place. She was followed in 1515 by Anne Westbrook, and then Elizabeth Rypose in 1523, the last abbess elected before the Dissolution of the abbey in 1539.

At this time John Foster was convent steward. He had a tenuous relationship through marriage with Sir Thomas Seymour, to whom the abbey was to be surrendered, and it was hoped that his influence might in some way soften the blow of complete dissolution. In the event the inevitable happened, but in 1554 the townspeople, who already had an unassailable right to use the north aisle of the abbey as their parish church, were able to purchase the whole church for one hundred pounds. Although the conventual buildings were destroyed, the church at least was saved.

Foundations of part of the pre-conquest abbey church apse were discovered in 1900 and are now generally agreed to belong to two periods. The lower part is of Edgar's time—967—with a later addition of around 1090. The whole comprises a wall five feet high which curves eastward between the western piers of the tower. It is all below the present floor level but a section of the flooring is removed to allow the public to see a part of it. Almost all the major work we see above ground belongs to the rebuilding which began around 1120 and continued into the thirteenth century. A Lady Chapel extended eastward but this was demolished. The tower, transepts, chancel and ambulatory, all of the early twelfth century remain.

I cannot claim to be an uncritical admirer of Norman art, but when I stand at the crossing of Romsey Abbey and look up at the richness of the mouldings and the ingenuity and skill of the carving, combined with the sheer majesty of the tiers of arches, the massive piers, and the vaulting, I am thrilled, for here may be found a rare peak of artistic achievement. However, ideas were changing and building continued as a new style formed, construction of the nave and aisles progressing westward over

Romsey Abbey from the north-west

a period of a little under a hundred years, and a gradual change from massive Norman work towards an elegance and lightness of touch is evident.

On the south side of the abbey, in the external angle between the transept and the nave aisle, is the Romsey Rood, a superb carving in stone of the crucified Christ, with the hand of God appearing below a cloud. The Christ does not show the agony of the Cross, as in later, medieval work, but is a Christ of majesty.

95

Romsey Abbey: the interior

The carving may have originally had the usual attendant figures of Mary and St John, but unlike many other similar images the Christ figure has escaped mutilation by the iconoclasts. The date of the work is open to much speculation—scholars have placed it at differing times in the eleventh century—but a period of within forty years before the Conquest, or shortly after, about 1075, has been suggested. In my opinion it retains far more Saxon feeling than Norman and must be the work of a Saxon sculptor even if it is post-Conquest. It is placed in a wall dated *c.* 1190. The fact that the church for which it was originally made is now rebuilt there can be no impelling reason why this sculpture should remain in its present exposed position. It is a work of immense artistic value—and beyond price—yet tourists rub their fingers over it, madmen could strike it, or spray it with an aerosol—there are those who might do these things. These perils apart, the weather is destroying the stone and deterioration has been rapid since I first saw it as a youth many years ago. Surely this work should receive the protection accorded to highly important works of art—this is not just a piece of church decoration.

Another limestone carving in the abbey, only two feet five inches high, is a crucified Christ with attendant figures and two soldiers. Above the arms of the cross are two angels. Similarities of this carving with the Winchester School of manuscripts have been claimed and it is traditionally believed to have been given to the abbey by Canute and dates from the second quarter of the eleventh century. It is above the altar in St Anne's Chapel.

The history and architectural qualities of the abbey may somewhat overshadow Romsey, but I am not prepared to join the ranks of writers who denigrate the town. I first visited it thirty-five years ago, and formed an attachment to it. It is a compact, busy town, and quite apart from the abbey, full of interest. It has a lively market, good shops and interesting streets. The River Test flows to the west of the centre and is therefore not an evident feature, but it can be seen in Mill Street where the old mill and its grounds have been very pleasantly laid out with ornamental gardens—including voracious trout in a stream for visitors to feed—by a firm selling equipment and materials for gardens and ornamental fish ponds.

Several good houses of various periods help to make the town attractive. The oldest house, known as King John's Hunting Lodge, is unfortunately tucked away down a path opposite the east end of the abbey and for this reason its importance was not realized until 1927. King John houses did not necessarily belong

Romsey on a busy Saturday afternoon

to that monarch, but because of his bad reputation his name became synonymous with the Devil and was applied to ancient buildings of unknown origin. The Romsey house is believed to date to the mid-thirteenth century—about 1230-40—and was a first-floor hall house. The ground floor of such a building was used as a store with the upper floor reached by an outside stair. At Romsey a fireplace and chimney were added in the fourteenth century, succeeding an open hearth, supported by a post from the ground with smoke finding its way out through a louvre in the roof. The hall was used as an eating and living room by the lord—or perhaps in this case, an official of the abbey. Other buildings would have been close, or attached to it—possibly a chapel, perhaps a private room—a solar, and as evidence shows, a covered outer stair. The roof is of crown post construction, but originally it is thought to have been composed only of coupled rafters and three tie beams. There are various incised medieval graffiti on the walls including shields and badges of certain noblemen believed to have been at Romsey with Edward I in February 1306. The original ownership of the house is unknown but at the Dissolution it belonged to the abbey and was acquired by John Foster, who may have lived there as chaplain to 'a chapel of St Andrew within the Infirmary'. Foster probably added the sixteenth-century timber-framed house, now contiguous with the hall, and lived there after the surrender of the abbey with his wife Jane Wadham, formerly the abbey sextoness. Foster's name appears again in connection with Baddesley Manor and one gets the impression that he, like certain noble lords, was making what he could out of the Dissolution.

Broadlands, the home of Lord Palmerston, and later Lord Mountbatten of Burma, stands to the south of the town and to the east of the River Test. The Broadlands estate is entered on the townside by a lodge designed by Nesfield in 1870 in a style typical of his work, using red brick, pargetting and tall chimneys. Broadlands was visited by James I but the house he knew, a single block with two long projecting wings on the east side was enlarged in 1767-8 by Lancelot (Capability) Brown and his son-in-law, Henry Holland. Brown filled in the area between the wings to create an east façade with a three-bay recessed loggia, and at the west, or garden front is a three-bay portico with a pediment rendered to simulate stone. Of the many notable interiors Holland was responsible for remodelling, the saloon of 1788, in a rather fussy style of decoration, is reminiscent of Adam. The house derives much attraction from its site near the river.

The Dolphin Hotel, Romsey

Perhaps the park and countryside east of Broadlands is well-named—broad, flat, and rather dull—and beyond the park the railway, the M27 and the urban expansion of Southampton. Nursling, now entangled in the M27, is where St Boniface, in the eighth century, set out from a Benedictine monastery on a

101

The statue of Palmerston, Romsey

site there known as The Walls, to convert north European tribes to Christianity. Named 'Winfrith' at birth, St Boniface was born in Crediton in 680. He entered the Benedictine abbey of Exeter as a boy, and later moved to Nursling to teach, where he became known as Boniface—doer of 'good things'.

Nursling church is at the end of a short road in a peaceful enclave just north of the M27, that runs to meadows, the River Test and power pylons. The church is mostly fourteenth century, restored by Street in 1881 and later by Kinnear Tarte in 1890, but there is evidence of thirteenth-century work, especially in the blocked arch south of the chancel arch. The proportions of the chancel arch, which is tall and narrow, have led to the suggestion that the church may have a Saxon origin: the connection with St Boniface certainly makes this supposition credible. In the south transept is a painted alabaster monument to Sir Richard Mille and his wife dated 1613, and in the churchyard the grave of O.G.S. Crawford, pioneer of aerial photo-

102

graphy. Opposite the church is a fine brick house, once the rectory, it looks late eighteenth century—perhaps 1775.

A mile from the church, east of the railway, is Grove Place, an attractive Elizabethan brick house at the end of a long drive. It was built for James Paget and had long projecting wings with octagonal turrets set in the re-entrant angles. The interior has several good stone fireplaces and plaster ceilings contemporary with its first build. Also typical of its period is a long gallery extending the full length of the house. Grove Place is now a school and not open to the public.

Rownhams, to the north of Nursling, is a Victorian village on the edge of a large development by the Southampton Local Authority. Further north is North Baddesley, where development has taken place to the south of the A37 leaving the old manor and church isolated about a mile to the north.

The Knights Hospitallers of Godsfield had a cell at North Baddesley to which they had transferred their headquarters by 1355. This is indicated by a document of that date which refers to a preceptor of North Baddesley. They were suppressed in 1536 and their preceptory has vanished. The present Baddesley Manor, a late eighteenth-century house, stands on the site. Thomas Foster, who assisted at the Dissolution of Romsey Abbey and purchased the confiscated manor of the Hospitallers from Sir Nicholas Throckmorton in 1553. Eventually the manor passed through marriage to Sir Thomas Fleming.

North Baddesley church stands upon a hill and overlooks a

A Knight Hospitaller

wide wooded landscape to the north. The church is small and very charming, the variety of materials with which it is built adding much to its attraction. The walls are of flint and stone and the low tower is of brick, dated 1674. The interior is simple with a screen inscribed 'T.F., 1602' and a pulpit of about the same date. The initials are of Sir Thomas Fleming of North Stoneham—a relative of Thomas Foster.

A tomb-chest on the north side of the nave is believed to be that of a Hospitaller, but outside in the churchyard is the more recent grave of Charles Smith. In 1822 Smith was hanged after conviction at Winchester Assizes for trying to avoid apprehension having shot and wounded under-keeper Robert Snelgrove on Lord Palmerston's estate. Palmerston attempted to prevent the execution but was unsuccessful.

7   The Villages of the Bourne and the Test

There cannot be a more delightful, idyllic river than the Test, or valley through which it flows. From its source at Ashe a small stream soon increases in size, its waters dividing and rejoining in numerous water courses as it flows along the wide valley. It develops into a considerable river around Longparish and increases greatly in width before it merges with the Itchen in Southampton Water.

The warmth of the water from the deep chalk encourages early growth in the spring and ensures a later lushness along its banks. Water life flourishes, especially the brown trout, and many claim it to be the finest trout stream in the world. It is certainly one of the most prestigious and the Houghton Club which manages a considerable length of the water is one of the most exclusive clubs. Founded in 1822, the Houghton Club is limited to seventeen members and at its headquarters in the Grosvenor Hotel at Stockbridge records are kept of every fish taken and the fly used.

From Romsey, upstream to Leckford and Fullerton where the River Anton joins the Test, the A3057 follows the east bank. From Wherwell the B3048 then passes on the western side to Hurstbourne Priors, where it leaves the Test to follow the valley of the Bourne. The B3400 from Andover continues through Whitchurch to Ashe near the source of the Test. With a few deviations these roads provide a good route to follow when exploring the upper valley.

North of Romsey near Awbridge is Stanbridge Earls, a stone house with two large and three smaller gables and now a school. The windows retain their original mullions and transoms of wood, and the porch, off-centre, is dated 1658. At the rear of the house there is evidence of the older building Roger Gollop of Southampton acquired with the manor in 1652—and which he rebuilt in six years.

On the east side of the valley at Timsbury a sixteenth-century rood screen and late Elizabethan pulpit are features of a small church with an unspoilt interior. At Michelmersh nearby thatched cottages, larger Georgian and early Victorian houses line the lanes leading to the church, which is well signposted. It has an impressive timber-framed tower, once detached, and although much restored in the nineteenth century the interior gives a sense of space. On the north side of the chancel are two monuments: a large tomb-chest with an effigy of a cross-legged knight, Sir Geoffrey de Canterton, Forester of the New Forest in *c.* 1320, and a small, attractive tablet with two kneeling figures, commemorating Tristram Funtleroy.

In 1201 Augustinian canons settled at Mottisfont on the western side of the valley and at the dissolution the priory was acquired by Lord Sandys who owned The Vyne at Basingstoke. He did not demolish the priory totally, but adapted it to domestic use, as did Thomas Wriothesley at Titchfield. The principal rooms are in the nave of the church and the drawing-room at the north end of the west range was decorated by Rex Whistler in 1938-9, his last major work before his death in the Second World War.

In Mottisfont parish church some good Norman work of the twelfth century includes the chancel arch. A memorial to William Sandys of 1628 shows he preferred to be buried on his own land rather than share his ancestors' tomb at The Vyne. Glass in the east window came from the Holy Ghost Chapel at Basingstoke.

Continuing upstream from Mottisfont, along the narrow lane on the west bank of the river or along the main A3037, from which may be seen the embankment of the old railway that ran between the Salisbury-Southampton line and the main London-Exeter line, we come to Bossington and Horsebridge. There are large brick mills at both places, and at Horsebridge the remains of an old railway station are in a state of picturesque decay. Here also the Roman road from Old Sarum and the lead mines of the Mendips crossed the Test to Winchester, its alignment passing near the old station. At this point in 1783 a pig of lead weighing nearly 156 pounds was found. Believed to have been lost on its way to Clausentum (Bitterne) for exportation, it bears an inscription dating it to the fourth consulate of Nero, AD 60–68. It is now in the British Museum.

A mile to the north-east Kings Somborne is a large scattered village with houses clustered along the lanes leading away from the main A3057. The fifteenth-century boundary banks of John of Gaunt's deer park are visible on the sloping ground between the river and the village, where a small stream is crossed by numerous bridges. Thatch is the traditional roofing material, with cob, flint and brick used for both houses and boundary walls. The church has been thoroughly restored and although the nave arcades are in part nineteenth century a section of the south arcade dates from the early thirteenth century and medieval graffiti may be found on one of the piers. Two large brasses on the chancel floor commemorate fourteenth-century Winchester merchants and are important to historians of medieval costume.

A little more than three miles to the east through Ashley, on Mount Down near Beacon Hill, is Farley Mount. This is a large Bronze Age barrow upon which stands a monument erected in remembrance of a horse being driven so hard in the chase that the rider, a member of the Paulet St John family, rode him at a chalk pit and a sheer drop of twenty-five feet. The horse landed safely, and it was he rather than the man who was renamed 'Beware Chalk Pit' and was put to race on Worthy Down within a year, where he won. The panoramic views from here make it a favourite place with townspeople from Winchester only four miles away.

Farley Chamberlayne church, a mile away almost due south and one of the most attractive churches in Hampshire, has few neighbours—only a farm, a house to the east which was once a school and a ruinous brick building associated with the naval telegraph that operated visually from London to Wessex. There are only traces on the ground of the deserted medieval village. The church has a Norman south door and a crown-post roof whose timber is a beautiful silver-grey. A sad monument in the chancel records the death of John St John in 1627 aged only twenty-four, also his wife aged twenty-three and their infant. The parents are shown holding the child in a wicker cradle. A large panelled tomb-monument of William St John, who died in 1609, has an effigy and a canopy supported on Ionic columns surmounted by an achievement panel.

From Farley Chamberlayne a maze of lanes lead to Upper Eldon and the redundant single-cell twelfth-century church of St John the Baptist. This was built in rendered flint rubble with stone door openings and quoins. It is remarkable that nine of the customary twelve consecration crosses remain—a large number for such a building. The east wall fell and was rebuilt in brick in the eighteenth century, while in the nineteenth century the chapel was reported to be used as a cowshed and again repaired.

Farley Chamberlayne church

By 1971, when it was once more dirty and neglected, the church was declared redundant and in 1973 was vested in the Redundant Churches Fund. Extensive repairs were carried out by the Fund in 1975. Often locked, a key has to be obtained before entering—a regrettable but necessary precaution.

The work done by the Redundant Churches Fund is beyond praise. To save a precious building because it is beautiful and can continue as a place of prayer and quietness is reason enough.

Little Somborne, in this locality, is a hamlet no less remote than Farley Chamberlayne and Upper Eldon and is surrounded by woodland. In early June the giant flowering chestnuts hum with the sound of bees and indeed it is a quiet enchanting place at any time of year. It is made especially attractive by a small church where Saxon foundations were recovered by Martin Biddle in association with Richard Sawyer of Winchester, architect to the Redundant Churches Fund. The foundations of the apsidal east end of the church were exposed and may be seen within the present building. The position of the apse prompted excavation at the west end where it was revealed that the foundations of the Saxon church extend further westward. This indicates that the pre-Conquest long and short work at the north-west corner of the present church is re-sited. A Saxon pilaster strip exists in the north wall with the lower section of a corresponding on in the south wall. H.M. Taylor in *Anglo-Saxon Architecture* (Volume III) expresses the opinion that although decorative, a pilaster strip is structural. The stones penetrate the thickness of the wall to upwards of twelve inches. This serves two purposes. Firstly most Saxon walls are constructed of rubble, and so the placing at intervals of stone pilaster strips assisted in the construction of straight upright walls. Secondly, a plaster strip confines the spread of any deterioration of the walling to an adjoining section.

Marshcourt stands on an elevated site on the east side of the Test valley, one mile south of Stockbridge. When Lutyens built the house in 1901-4, for Herbert Johnson, he used the materials

The restored Saxon church at Little Somborne

of the landscape. The house of hard chalk, flint, clay tiles and brick is at one with the site, and the random use of small panels of flint, adding an accent to large wall areas, is a device that worked well in Lutyens' hands but was later used *ad nauseam* and to poorer effect by lesser men. The exterior, in a free Tudor style, is imaginative and contrasts with the Classical interior reminiscent of Wren. The doorway of the main porch, typical of Lutyens' inexhaustible ingenuity and genius, has long key-stones sloping inwards from an outer arch to an inner one which leads to a tunnel of chequered tile. The house is now a school and not open to the public.

Across the river at Houghton a lane leads from the long village street up to the church, the red-brick vicarage and the Manor House. Slender oak posts carry the west bell-turret, and the crown-post roof in the nave looks original. Stone brackets on the capitals of the south arcade indicate the position of an earlier aisle roof, an interesting detail which compares with Damerham church, where the original aisle roof is in place. Northwards outside the village is Houghton Lodge in the cottage orné style.

Broughton stands two miles away on the Wallop Brook, a western tributary of the Test close to the Roman road from Winchester to Old Sarum. The church is Norman and has a north arcade of the early thirteenth century with round piers and scalloped capitals—the arches are late enough to be pointed. A circular brick pigeon house of the seventeenth century, which must replace an earlier one, is unusually sited in the churchyard. In medieval England a lord of the manor alone was privileged to keep pigeons, a vital source of winter meat. Could this be an instance of a fourteen-century lord of the manor being the lay rector with a vicar or a curate?

A very early Baptist chapel was established in the village in 1655 during the period of the commonwealth: being founded in Holland only in 1609 it is surprising that the Baptists should have arrived in a small Hampshire village so soon.

Harmony Hall was built between Broughton and East Tytherley in 1839 by Robert Owen, an early industrialist turned philanthropist who established a community to live out the ideals of socialism. The experiment worked for a time, but funds ran out and the project had failed by 1845. Harmony Hall then became a school, Queenwood College, with an 'advanced' approach to education adopted by the Quaker headmaster. The school closed in 1895 and a few years later the house was severely damaged by fire.

Returning again to the river a raft-like causeway of compressed chalk, laid down in the remote past, crosses the valley at Stockbridge, a town which grew in importance before the railway age, when the Welsh drovers rested there on their way eastwards. An inscription in Welsh on a house in Houghton Road which was once an inn, offers good hay for beasts and ale and a bed in the hay for drovers.

The size of the town may deceive the visitor as it is little more than a single row of buildings on each side of the wide main street, in the past frequently congested by sheep markets and fairs. A mixture of cottages and small houses are interspersed with pleasant, unpretentious buildings, including the town hall of brick dated 1810, while the Grosvenor Hotel of about 1800 has a large porch with an upper room supported on columns extending into the wide roadway. The White Hart at the eastern end of the main street has extensive stabling and was an important staging post. Nearby the surviving chancel of the old church, a chapelry of King's Somborne, is a forlorn little building in a large churchyard containing many tombstones, one commemorating John Buckett of the King's Head who died in 1802. A much quoted inscription that makes play on Buckett's name commences,

> 'And is alas! Poor Buckett gone?
> Farewell, convivial honest John,
> Oft at the well by fatal stroke
> Buckets—like   pitchers—must   be
> broke.'

Stockbridge or White Somborne—*Sumburne* in the Domesday Book—has a long history as borough and manor. The manor, always a royal possession, passed to John of Gaunt by marriage. John of Gaunt's deer park can be traced on the ground near King's Somborne—and thus it remained until purchased by Joseph Foster Barham in 1824. Events befell the manor which subsequently led to its being pawned and bought by a London firm. In the 1920s to the subsequent advantage of all, Norman Hill, solicitor, retired to Stockbridge, and purchased land carrying conditions that included his taking the manor of Stockbridge. This he did. Following his death, the manor passed briefly to his son, and then on his death to his sister, Professor Rosemary Hill, who vested it in the National Trust in 1947. At the time of writing Professor Hill continues, as a

The Grosvenor Hotel, Stockbridge

representative of the Trust, to act with charm and still in the capacity of Lord of the Manor she presides at the courts. The power of the court now reduced, it nevertheless still holds jurisdiction over land within the manor during the grazing season

112

and over the sheep run on Stockbridge Down. Geese are not allowed to graze the manorial meadows.

The origin of Stockbridge as a borough is unknown but Elizabeth I gave right of representation in Parliament in 1563. By the late seventeenth century corruption was evident and a bill of disenfranchisement almost succeeded. As late as 1790 Captain Luttrell and Lord Inham spent ten thousand pounds each on an election, but this most corrupt of corrupt boroughs lost its status by the Reform Bill of 1832.

Over many decades racing provided a diversion between the intervals of election rivalry and brought money and visitors to the town. Edward VII, as Prince of Wales, enjoyed the races and was a frequent visitor at Hermit Lodge on the Houghton road. The racecourse below Danebury, where the grandstand can still be seen two miles from the village was reached from a lane off the A30 Salisbury road.

Also on the Salisbury road almost opposite Houghton Down Farm are remnants of a base used by military airships during the Great War. Dane Hill Fort should also be visited to see the defended main entrance and the three lines of defence—the middle banks date to 1000 BC.

West of Danebury and reached along a lane from the A30 are the three Wallops on the Wallop Brook. All are attractive, but Middle Wallop has suffered from being on the main Salisbury to Andover road. Over and Nether Wallop have rows of thatched cottages, many in Nether Wallop rebuilt after serious fires in the seventeenth and eighteenth centuries. Thatched cob walls with corner arbours surround a small private garden in Over Wallop, one of the most enchanting gardens I have seen, demonstrating the charm of cob walls properly maintained. The Air Arm of the British Army and the Museum of Army Flying are near Middle Wallop, with an entrance from the A343.

Returning to Stockbridge and the Test a minor road follows the west side of the valley to Longstock, a typical Test village with thatched cottages lining the main street, the broach spire of the church adding a picturesque note. The unusual name of the inn the Peat Spade, originates from the digging of peat nearby and this could have a bearing on the story that the Test was navigable by the shallow draught ships of invading Danes. It is believed—with less conviction now than formerly—that they established a quay at Longstock where a channel may be seen in the meadows, but it could equally be the result of peat digging.

Joshua East acquired Longstock Park in 1849, and his sons

Steadman Memorial Baptist Chapel, Stockbridge

inherited. Their wish was to be buried at their favourite spot on the estate. This was done, and their graves are marked by a small enclosure where a track on Hazel Down crosses the lane from Longstock to Goodworth Clatford. This area was purchased by John Spedan Lewis in 1945. The gardens of Longstock are cared for as in the days of the East family and are open for the public on one Sunday afternoon a month in summer.

114

Leckford church, with a small weatherboarded bell-turret and walls of flint which have been rendered and much repaired, has an unaligned chancel and nave so placed to allow space for processions between the church and the churchyard boundary, an indication of the importance placed upon this aspect of ritual by the medieval church. On the western side of the valley a mile from the A303 Barton Stacey church, where space at the west end was restricted, may be compared in this respect. The medieval altar stone bearing five consecration crosses which was removed to the sanctuary pavement during the Reformation, was restored to its former use in 1921. The Jacobean pulpit has an octagonal sounding board with pendants at the angles— it bears initials 'R.S., I.H.', thought to be those of churchwardens at the time of its installation. A late twelfth-century Purbeck marble font is decorated with blank arcading in low relief.

Along the main road northwards from Leckford occasional glimpses may be had of the old railway built on the alignment of the former Andover canal, and beyond the point where the main road takes a sharp left turn, the railway divides with a branch line up the valley. The platforms of the station, Fullerton Junction, survive, as do several railway cottages, and here the Anton joins the Test near the Mayfly Inn, formerly the Seven Stars.

The lane which leaves the main road at this corner leads to Chilbolton—a village of great charm contrasting sharply with a great 'dish' some eighty feet across and other scientific hardware built at the old airfield on Chilbolton Down in 1967. At the north-eastern end of the village street superb thatch covers the extensive roofs and gables of a larger house and adjoining cottages. First impressions I find linger longest, and I never forget first seeing this village one bright sunny spring evening when the daffodils were at their best and were massed in gardens and on the verges of the village street.

The church stands in a large churchyard and has Norman origins. The chancel is thirteenth century, and the aisles are fourteenth, but the south-west tower and spire are Victorian— constructed of wood and stone in 1893. Inside a Jacobean pulpit and also a restored fifteenth-century screen may be seen.

Opposite the church, to the east, the rectory is a chequered brick building, early seventeenth century, altered about 1700. It adds greatly to the village by providing a note of elegant Classical brick to contrast with vernacular timber and thatch of smaller cottages.

Chilbolton

From Chilbolton it is but a mile across the valley to Wherwell, the sister settlement which with justifiable pride is claimed by many to be the most beautiful of the Test Valley villages, where thatched timber-framed cottages are grouped in the wooded valley which here amid lush growth the river divides into many channels.

116

Wherwell, the site chosen by a queen who sought to ease her conscience by founding a nunnery, is connected with a story of violence and deception. It relates that King Edgar sent a courtier to report upon the fabled beauty of Aelfthryth, a daughter of the Earl of Devon, but the untruthful messenger married the lady himself. His deceit was discovered and Edgar murdered him while out hunting in Harwood Forest between Wherwell and Longparish. The lady then willingly married Edgar and gave him a son, Ethelred. Upon Edgar's death twelve years later his son, Edward, by a previous marriage, succeeded his father only to meet his death four years later at Corfe Castle, stabbed by his stepmother. Ethelred took the crown but he proved to be one of our least successful monarchs. Repentant, his mother entered her nunnery at Wherwell. Wherwell Priory was granted to Lord de la Warr following the Dissolution, and with various complications in the inheritance it remained with the family until 1695. Lord de la Warr was made Governor of Virginia in 1606 and then later founded his own colony of Delaware named after him.

A diversion may be taken here, as north of Wherwell one of the channels of the Test is joined by the Dever—or North Brook—which has its source at East Stratton. Travelling eastward, Barton Stacey has been mentioned in connection with Leckford church and its unusual plan—the sixteenth-century tower with tall pinnacles and high stair turret being built partly within the nave to allow the passage of processions at a point where the closeness of the churchyard boundary allowed little space. The east end of this church is also unusual, with the two eastern piers of the nave arcades carrying the chancel arch, arches eastward into the nave and arches across the aisles.

The old house near Wonston church—the former rectory, stuccoed and Georgian—hides a medieval hall house. Altered within, the medieval hall, cross passage, and low end with buttery and pantry can be recognized. The hall is no longer 'open' but has an inserted floor, and the roof is not original.

To the north on the A30 is Cranbourne Farm, which stands near traces of a moat and is possibly the site of Cranbourne Manor House. Norton Manor House is to the north, near Upper Bullington, and is a good early eighteenth-century brick and flint house with a wide eaves cornice typical of its date. There are brick pilasters at the corners with moulded capitals which have yellow and blue Dutch tiles set in the necking.

Stoke Charity church is notable for its interior, but not only does it have a massive Norman pier in its two-bay north arcade,

Wherwell

it is also full of monuments. The sculpture known as the Mass of St Gregory, although mutilated by age, is a remarkable survival of the late fifteenth century. It shows Christ revealed to two kneeling figures at Mass. When images were being smashed by order of Edward VI this was saved by fixing it to the wall, facing inwards.

Micheldever gives its name to the once great oak wood that extended westward to the Candovers and was said by William Cobbett to be the finest in England. Micheldever church was damaged by fire and George Dance built a brick octagonal nave east of the surviving sixteenth-century tower. Monuments inside the church recall the Baring family, bankers and land-owners in the district, with residences at The Grange and Stratton Park. Micheldever Station called Andover Road Station until the construction of the Popham Tunnel, is two miles to the north of the village and was a terminus of the future London-Southampton railway. Designed by Sir William Tite in 1840 as a prestige feature, the opening ceremony was held there that year. Difficulties in building the tunnel at Popham and in making cuttings through the chalk from Oakley had delayed the link with the line at Basingstoke from Nine Elms.

Returning to the Test, above Wherwell the group of hamlets Forton, Middleton, Longparish and East Aston comprise the present parish of Longparish—formerly Middleton—and extend along the main streams of the Test. The church at Middleton is early thirteenth century in origin, the nave arcades have round piers and scalloped capitals supporting pointed arches, but one capital—on the south side—has stiff-leaf foliage. The sixteenth-century west tower is of chequered flint and stone. The reputed spot in Harwood Forest where Earl Athelwold was slain by King Edgar in 963 is in the parish—Deadman's Black Copse—westward along a lane from Middleton and marked by a monument erected in 1826. Longparish had a station on the branch railway known as 'The Nile' and part of the vintage film *The Ghost Train* was shot near the village in the 1920s.

Above Longparish the valley widens out considerably and the river passes out of sight from the road which turns north and leads to Hurstbourne Priors on the Bourne, a tributary of the Test. Referred to as Down Husband by William Cobbett, Hurstbourne Priors has a cricket ground overlooked by the church tower, built in 1870—'neo-Norman and deplorably late' is how one writer described it. I like it. From a distance especially, the colour is warm and mellow in a western evening light. Inside the church is a monument to Sir Robert Oxenbridge, Constable of the Tower and Lord of the Manor from 1558 until his death in 1574. His descendants held the manor until they sold in 1636 to the Wallop family, who were later, in 1743, created Earls of Portsmouth. Their nineteenth-century mansion in the park, demolished in 1965, replaced an earlier house by James Wyatt. It was recorded in 1660 by the Dean and Chapter of Winchester 'that they may rebuild their demolished cloisters, library, dwelling house, etc.' of timber from Hurstbourne Park—the Chapter House and cloisters having been pulled down by Bishop Horne in the 1560s. This work was not carried out, but repairs to the cathedral roof were undertaken at this time.

St Mary Bourne, on the Bourne a little further upstream beyond the railway viaduct and the watercress beds, was a pioneer of street lighting with oil-lamps—the last surviving lamp was rescued and restored to commemorate the present Queen's Jubilee. Standing close to the village street, the church of flint and stone combines with the thatched cottages and small bridge across the Bourne to create a memorable scene,

The viaduct at St Mary Bourne

while in the churchyard to the east sheep are grazed in the summer months. The interior is no less rewarding where one of the four Hampshire Tournai fonts may be seen, this one considered to be particularly fine, as one of the panels is decorated with doves and the others with vines.

Leaving the Bourne for the present and returning to the Test, the White Hart at Whitchurch stands at what was once the junction of the Newbury to Southampton and Exeter to London coach systems, and many travellers have passed through the entrance which is unusually placed on a corner of the building. Opposite is the town hall, a graceful building in Georgian brick with pediment and cupola.

A busy small town, Whitchurch has gained from putting the river to work. Water power from the Test assisted the development of two unusual industries—silk weaving in Whitchurch itself, and just outside the town, paper manufacture for banknotes at Laverstock.

The Whitchurch silk mill is near the town centre, off the Winchester road. Erected in the eighteenth century and constructed of chalk blocks faced with brick, it replaced an earlier building and is a charming example of industrial architecture at its best. The pediment with a clock and the graceful cupola were added in 1815 to commemorate the Battle of Waterloo. Sophisticated machinery accurately governing the waterwheel is restored to its original state, although power is now provided

120

by electricity. A mill has been on the site since the Domesday Survey, at one time a brush-making factory, later a woollen mill, and about 1845 silk was introduced by the Bingham family. Soon after 1900 the Hide family continued the weaving of silk. This was at first used in insulation coverings by the electrical industry, but when superseded by plastic the mill began weaving the finest silk threads from China. The fine silk is now used in ceremonial dress for lawyers and academics—and beautiful clothes for ladies. A shop at the mill is open to the public. It was recently announced that the mill would cease manufacture, however the Hampshire Buildings Preservation Trust has acquired the building and will ensure its preservation.

The manufacture of banknote paper on the Test has long been associated with the Portal family, and now a large company employs over a thousand workers. Henry de Portal came to England as a Huguenot refugee, was apprenticed to a papermaker at South Stoneham on the River Itchen and in 1711 applied for naturalization. He soon made influential friends, especially the Heathcote family of Hursley who assisted him in acquiring Bere Mill, where he started making high quality paper. Through Sir Gilbert Heathcote, Governor of the Bank of England, he obtained a contract in 1727 to supply paper for banknotes. The mill soon moved to Laverstoke where the business remained until 1950, although by 1922 it also opened a mill near Overton Station, still its present home. The 1727 contract is still operative.

At Freefolk the crescent of thatched cottages built by Lord Portal in 1939 has been called 'a little ridiculous': it is a pity there are not more buildings as 'ridiculous' as these. They are well designed and attractive, composing well as a group. Opposite a lane leads to the old church and parsonage built in 1858 by G.E. Street in flint and brick—one of his best smaller houses. The church, now cared for by the Redundant Churches Fund, is a small single-cell. There is nothing grand about it—its simplicity is its charm. The large parish church behind the thatched cottages by J.L. Pearson in 1896 is quite the opposite, its attraction being the richness of its decoration. Laverstock Park, the home of the Portal family, built in 1796-8 by Joseph Bonomi upon rising ground north of the A3400, is of ochre colour brick which harmonizes with the landscape. The architectural composition lives up to its beautiful site and the grand Ionic portico effectively adds charm and character to the scene.

As at New Alresford, Bishop de Lucy of Winchester built a 'new' town on a grid plan on the southern side of the Test,

The White Hart Hotel, Whitchurch

leaving the old town of Overton, with church and manor house, on the northern side. The 'new' town of 1200 retains the original plan of two streets parallel to the wide main street and two crossing at right angles. A large cottage of cruck construction at Southington on the edge of the town was almost destroyed by fire in 1980 and rebuilt at once.

The church has been thoroughly restored but fortunately the timber construction of the chancel roof remains—stylistically important and probably late thirteenth century. Court Farm House and barn, at the bishop's demesne farm to the west of the church, are of interest. The house contains a robing room used by the visiting bishops.

At Quidhampton a fragment of a Norman chapel partly concealed among farm buildings can be seen from the road, and at Polhampton the farmhouse built of brick—probably in the mid-1600s—has a moulded cornice of brick and mullion windows. Near here close to Ashe church, a small building of flint, restored about 1870 by G. G. Scott Junior, is the source of the Test fed by a spring from beneath the chalk. Berrydown Court on the B3400 between Ashe and Overton is a private residence, not open to the public and only the entrance on the road may be seen, but it is by Lutyens and even the sight of a fragment of his work is rewarding.

Ashe is two miles from Steventon—Jane Austen's family home—and the lane from her village meets the Overton-Basingstoke road opposite another lane from Deane. At this place one can imagine her boarding the coach at the crossroads. She died in 1817 and although she knew Deane House the church was not built until 1818. A complete Gothic Revival church as yet untouched, Deane church makes a fine group with the house. I recall that a year or two ago one of the pinnacles was removed from the tower for repairs and could be examined closely: it was undoubtedly Coade Stone.

8   Andover and the North-West

A crescent-shaped area bounded by the county border to the west and north and a line from Wiltshire through Quarley, Abbotts Ann, Andover, Hurstbourne Tarrant, Hannington and Wolverton to Berkshire, contains the high lands of the chalk downs and a part of the region of the younger rocks. It contains some of the greatest contrasts of landscape in the county.

The impressive Quarley Hill is south of the A303 and under certain light conditions Bronze Age boundary ditches meeting on the summit are visible at a distance. The site was excavated in 1938 by Professor Christopher Hawkes of the Faculty of Archaeology at Oxford, and he proved that the ditches had been cut across the hill between 100 and 500 BC. They belong to a series of earthworks in the Bourne Valley thought to have been boundaries to land holdings. Later Iron Age ramparts cut through these ditches and an Iron Age palisade was erected on the vallum of the rampart. The reason for such a fortified place—which was never completed—is not known. However, there is evidence that imminent danger threatened the region, as similar uncompleted fortifications have been found—at Ladle Hill to the north-east near Litchfield for example.

In the 1930s a group of houses known as Hugh's Settlement was built below the northern face of Quarley Hill by the architect Jessica Albury. She chose a variant of the traditional cob method and used chalk mixed with straw and water moulded into blocks. These were bonded with 'mortar' composed only of chalk and water—the individual blocks can be identified in the roof spaces where they have not been plastered. The blocks are irregular in size and larger than bricks.

Quarley church contains Saxon work of the eleventh century—the Saxon-Norman overlap period. The nave, constructed in flint-laid herring-bone fashion, is Saxon. Its age may be ascertained by the evidence of three windows, two of which

Quarley church, north-west Hampshire

are blocked but clearly the work of a Saxon mason. There is also a blocked Saxon north doorway. A Venetian east window in the chancel replaces an earlier window and has the inscription 'Guliemvs Benson and Henricus Hoare FAD, 1723' on the outside, and repeated inside with the names reversed. Possibly one of the first Venetian windows in an ecclesiastic setting in England, it would have been very modern and startling in 1719—perhaps a public demonstration of a commitment to the principles of Palladian architecture? William Benson built his own house, Wilbury House in Wiltshire in 1710, and Henry Hoare Senior employed Colin Campbell to build Stourhead, also

125

in Wiltshire. Both men were ardent admirers of Palladio and it is interesting therefore that Henry Hoare's son was Lord of the Manor of Quarley in 1719.

Amport, east of Quarley, has a large church in the Decorated style—unusual in Hampshire—in which there is a small alabaster panel, said to be fifteenth century, of a head of John the Baptist with saints, a Christ risen from the tomb and angels—an unusual piece. The RAF occupy Amport House, built in the nineteenth century after the Elizabethan mansion was destroyed by fire. Lutyens designed the garden terraces and also the gate piers which have a touch of his genius—and his whimsy. At Monxton nearby an eighteenth-century parson, Thomas Rothwell devoted to mathematics, employed a curate to minister to his flock and did not enter his church for years. Rothwell's church went when Woodyer rebuilt it in 1854.

A gate pier by Lutyens at Amport House, Amport

Weyhill was the scene of the great autumn fair where, according to Defoe, 'a prodigious quantity of sheep' were sold.

Horses also were brought for auction, and there was a cheese market and a motley collection of sideshows. It was a Weydon Priors (Weyhill Fair) in a booth selling 'fumity', an unpalatable, bland broth made agreeable by adding rum, that Henchard, in Thomas Hardy's *The Mayor of Casterbridge* sold his wife and child for five guineas in a mock auction conducted by the man 'with a damp voice, and eyes like buttonholes'. Hardy lists the attractions which brought visitors in: 'peepshows, toy stands, waxworks, inspired masters, disinterested medical men who travelled for the public good, thimble-riggers, nicknack-vendors and readers of Fate'.

Abbotts Ann south of Weyhill is interesting for the survival of the custom of 'maiden garlands'. Each of the many garlands and paper gloves hanging in the church were carried at the funeral of a bachelor of good repute or spinster born in the parish. This form of tribute was not unique to Abbotts Ann: Shakespeare refers to the garland for the dead Ophelia as a 'crant' and Gilbert White recorded their use at Selborne. I find it a moving and beautiful tradition, but the sight of so many garlands hanging from the nave walls is a sharp reminder of one's mortality.

The church is of brick, built in 1716 by Thomas 'Diamond' Pitt, so-called because he sold an exceptionally large diamond at great profit to the Regent of France who mounted it in the French crown.

Tradition may die hard at Abbotts Ann, a quiet place with cottages dotted along winding lanes. Cob-walling and thatched roofs are common, but flint and brick with timber-framing—there is at least one fine cruck cottage—is also to be found. In contrast, Andover nearby changed considerably following agreement that it should become an area of expansion, both of population and industry. New road networks like the maze of King Minos encircle the town, and estates—industrial and housing—appear incongruously in the landscape. Fortunately a modern town centre has not been imposed as it was at Basingstoke—much of the old town remains. Through traffic has been discouraged, which is good. In a visit to Andover one can therefore take pleasure in seeing many good buildings, at least this is my impression now, but in 1908 an author said of the town, 'Little else than tradition remains of old Andover.'

The town hall built in 1826 in the Greek Doric style dominates the High Street to good effect. On both sides of the wide road in front of it are a number of nineteenth-and early twentieth-century buildings which together produce a pleasing town centre. The Star and Garter—now the Danebury Hotel—is early nineteenth

127

Andover Town Hall

century, stuccoed, and with a good substantial porch. Old inns with yards remain: The George, The Globe and, where the High Street narrows and is paved, The Angel Inn. They lack the smells of hay and horses of eighty years ago which they will never have again, but they also lack the wall-creeper which was a feature of the buildings in times past. This they could still have and be all the better for it.

Andover was a lively place at election time. The George is reported as being mainly involved 'where most of the guineas changed hands and where most free drinks were handed to the incorruptibles'.

Beyond The Angel is a Norman arch from the old church. It was saved by Dr Goddard, a retired headmaster of Winchester College, who went to Andover as vicar in 1809 and rebuilt the parish church at his own expense. His architect was Augustus Livesay, and they studied the Early English style at first hand to enable them to produce this fine church. Work started in 1840 and was completed by 1846, but there were structural difficulties which Sydney Smirke corrected. The siting of the church is fortunate and the tall tower oversails the town to good effect.

The Old Vicarage nearby is early Georgian with pediment and Ionic porch. In New Street the museum is in the former headmaster's house, next to the Old Grammar School. It was built about 1750 in red brick and has an original doorcase and stair—the sashes also may be original. Jane Austen knew the house and visited the headmaster and his family. In East Street there are several early eighteenth-century houses and an 1830 chapel with a Tuscan porch—it is a very pleasant building.

A Norman arch from the old church at Andover

A plaque records the rebuilding in 1753 of the town mill in the south-west quarter of the town. It is now a restaurant—a once-venerated building now sacrificed to the present needs of modern society.

From Andover to Newbury the road passes pleasant country to the village of Enham Alamein—before the last war Enham Village Settlement—where some sixty years ago a training-centre and workshops were established for soldiers disabled in war, and a wide range of goods is produced.

Beyond Enham, through Doles Wood and at the bottom of Hurstbourne Hill, is Hurstbourne Tarrant, one of William

Andover: a view of St Mary's

Cobbett's favourite villages. He referred to it by its old name, Uphusband, and near the bridge at the bottom of Hurstbourne Hill was The Rookery, the home of his friend Joseph Blount.

Near here also was the home of the American artist Anna Lea Merritt who painted *Love Locked Out*, a picture in the Tate Gallery. Her cottage has been replaced by another house, but

130

her studio still stands in the garden. She wrote and illustrated *A Hamlet in Old Hampshire*, published in 1902, in which she describes the village with great affection and a little bewilderment.

The church stands in the village street near the Bourne rivulet with the side of the valley rising behind it. It has a weather-boarded bell-turret: 'the tower was erected in 1897, partly of old timbers', according to the *Victoria County History of Hampshire*. These 'old timbers' are painted and another source suggests that they were from a rood screen. The church contains a mixture of styles, the south doorway late Norman, the north arcade thirteenth century, the south a little earlier, and a western bay added in the fourteenth century. During the restoration in the 1880s the chancel was restored, and the flint walls of the nave refaced. Fourteenth-century wall-paintings in the north aisle—well-preserved rather than repainted—depict the three quick and the three dead. Another painting shows the deadly sins.

In the churchyard, near the south-west entrance, is a large memorial slab to Richard Martin, whose daughter married a Blount. I have been told that the stone was large and laid flat so that children could play marbles on it.

West of the church Parsonage Farm has a Georgian front on an earlier house, as well as brick gate piers dated 1685 and an impressive range of barns.

The Bladon Gallery on the A343 in a converted chapel was

Hurstbourne Tarrant

opened in 1949 by the late Mrs Doris Bladon-Hawton and was successful for many years as a gallery and 'workshop' for artists, but at the time of writing the gallery is closed.

Northward from Hurstbourne Tarrant the landscape rises to the high chalk downs and either the lane to Ibthorpe or to Faccombe will lead to these uplands—and to Combe. East and West Woodhay and Inkpen are all outside the county, 'given' to Berkshire for bureaucratic convenience. I have driven through these lanes on a late spring evening and not met another person. The drive to Netherton through a rich green dry valley is as enchanting as Netherton itself, with a thatched cottage, a farm-house, farm-buildings and a churchyard where St Michael's Church once stood. A large and very fine early Georgian brick house built as the rectory, completes the group. This was once an important centre, and foundations of a sequence of rebuilds of a large medieval manor house have been excavated. Beyond Netherton I drove taking turnings as I fancied. The road took me to the county boundary before Combe and the chalk down-land was all around me. I turned back across the side of a chalk spur to Linkenholt, then to Vernham Dean with a Jacobean manor house and a church restored by a curate who kept only the late Norman doorway. Then I came down to Ibthorpe, a hamlet of thatched cottages and Georgian farmhouses where Jane Austen stayed with her friends the Lloyds.

Crux Easton is east of the A343 Newbury road along a turning at the Three Legged Cross, a public house until the 1950s. The village is remote, and perhaps for this reason it was chosen as a suitable place to detain Sir Oswald Mosley during the 1939-45 war. The church was built in 1775 to replace a Norman building. Restored in 1894, demolition not restoration was what the vicar of the time wanted: he hoped for a 'better, and more church-like building'. Fortunately he did not have his way. Entered through a wrought-iron gate of fine quality the small churchyard con-tains a delightful small church of brick with arched windows in the nave and one large arched window in the chancel apse. The interior fittings are particularly good, there is marble pavement and panelling with pilasters in the apse, and the pulpit and lectern are also contemporary with the church.

An early pioneer in crop improvement, one Edward Lisle bought an estate at Crux Easton in 1692. He made notes on local agricultural practice and a book, *Observations in Husbandry*, based upon his work was published by his son in 1757. A copy is preserved at the Winchester Public Library. Edward Lisle had twenty children and nine of his daughters made a grotto for which Alexander Pope wrote an inscription starting 'This radiant pile of nine rural sisters raise'. Nothing remains of the grotto, but in the 1950s a few bricks were found in Grotto Copse where it is believed to have been built.

Ashmanworth, to the west of the A343, has a very unusual church with a mid-twelfth century nave and a slightly later chancel. The chancel arch is narrow and a squint has been cut on either side at a later date. Wall-paintings, perhaps twelfth century, together with thirteenth-century pantings for a rood, cover the wall between nave and chancel. There is a brick porch of 1694 and the east wall of the chancel is brick, dated 1745. A bell-turret at the west is carried on a frame within the nave.

Highclere and Burghclere jointly, as Clere, were manors of the Bishops of Winchester who had a palace at Highclere, Clere being described in 1086 by the Domesday Survey as held by the Bishop of Winchester for the support of the monks of Winchester. The manor was exchanged in 1551 for land elsewhere when Edward VI received it from Bishop Poynet, and although briefly returned to the See of Winchester by Mary it had reverted to lay ownership by 1559. In the 1770s Capability Brown laid out the park at Highclere for Henry Herbert, Earl of Carnarvon, and Cobbett described it as 'the prettiest I have ever seen'. The house at that time, a large Classical mansion, was remodelled by Sir Charles Barry for the third earl in 1839-42 in an Elizabethan style. The park is not open to the public.

Newtown, one and a half miles north of Burghclere, was a mesne borough of the Bishop of Winchester—a town planned, as at Overton and Alresford, with burgage plots. The new village of 'Sandelford' first appears in accounts in 1218 and received a licence to hold a market in that year and the borough prospered. It recovered from the ravages of the Black Death but in the sixteenth century was described as a 'decayed borough'. The bishopric sold it the following century and it passed to the Earls of Carnarvon.

The fifth earl, who led the expedition and discovered the tomb of Tutankhamun with Howard Carter, is buried on Beacon Hill, but I think my interest lies more at Burghclere in the Sandham Memorial Chapel where from 1927-32 Stanley Spencer painted the interior with scenes derived from sketches he made while serving in Macedonia as a medical orderly. I was privileged to have frequently met Stanley Spencer when I was a student at the Slade School. To listen to him talk of art and everyday things with simplicity and enthusiasm was to glimpse,

The Schoolhouse, Upper Clatford, near Abbotts Ann

through him, a world of wonderment that only a brilliant mind could convey with so much childlike understanding and excitement. I doubt if he concerned himself too much with the 'isms' of art—he had his own vision of the world and he was driven to put it on canvas. His was a very personal art, he followed no one, and no one could follow him. How moving are his paintings at Burghclere, and how clearly has the utter futility, waste—and boredom—of war been proclaimed!

In the west of the Vale of Clere the largest village, Kingsclere, was a royal manor. In the twelfth century Henry I granted it to the Canons of St Mary, Rouen and they held it until the wars with France in the fourteenth century. Freemantle, an area to the south of Kingsclere, was a favourite royal park much frequented by King John, Henry III and other kings, until the seventeenth century when the property passed into a variety of ownerships and was farmed. A navy surveyor reported on the park in 1650 and it is perhaps surprising, even in this wooded countryside, that 437 oak trees were fit for use by the navy.

There are a number of good eighteenth-century houses in Kingsclere, particularly in Swan Street. The church is a little disappointing as it was very vigorously restored in 1848. It was originally a Norman building with a tower at the crossing. The north door and south chapel remain unspoilt and some monuments survive, particularly a large black and white marble and alabaster memorial to Sir Henry and Lady Bridget Kingsmill. This was erected by the widowed Lady Bridget in 1670—Sir Henry died in 1625, Lady Bridget in 1672.

Watership Down to the south has been made famous by Richard Adams, and on Ladle Hill is an Iron Age fort unfinished by its builders. In the nineteenth century John Porter, at his Kingsclere stables, trained six Derby winners on the turf of these downs, and today Ian Balding continues the tradition: his most famous winner of recent years was Mill Reef.

Wolverton church, along a lane off the A339, is medieval with a baroque outer shell of red brick and stone. The retention of the medieval church resulted in a low nave relative to the tower, and the architect built a tall gable between the nave and chancel to give height. The transepts and the east wall of the chancel are boldly treated with high-stepped gables containing deep niches—a truly baroque design attributed to Wren and worthy of him, but lacking documentary confirmation.

Three miles from Wolverton along lanes south-west of the A339, is Hannington. It is an attractive village with a large green in front of the church to which restorations and a western extension made in the nineteenth century, together with medieval work, make the survival of Saxon masonry unexpected. The walls of the nave of flint and stone rubble may be Saxon, but quoins at the north-east angle of the nave, set in long-and-short fashion, are of megalithic size and pre-Conquest.

Corner Cottage, Monxton

9 The North-East

Basingstoke was described by Brian Vesey-Fitzgerald as 'modern and proud of it', but he was writing before 1949. During the last war the town was a busy place, its metal foundries, heavy engineering and motor works making a considerable contribution and by the 1950s the population had grown to around twenty thousand. In the 1960s a Town Development Scheme, agreed jointly by the governing authorities of London, Basingstoke and Hampshire, was planned to attract firms to the town. Roads, housing and amenities were to be provided. Rapid development followed—skyscraper office blocks and a shopping-precinct near the centre were built by sacrificing some of the town's best architecture. Housing developments and industrial estates sprang up and a new road system was constructed. The new shopping development and attendant buildings demonstrate how unpleasant modern architecture can be and contrasts sharply with what remains of the old town, where there is variety and quality.

An exit from the new development can be made into Church Street where there is a small group of houses recently restored—one has a fragment of brickwork in a style of about 1630.

West of the church is Church Cottage, a timber-framed building, part jettied: it has a fine doorway, the entrance to the Old Vicarage. A section to the right of the doorway was known as the 'Vicarial Barn', and later the 'Malt House'. In 1865 part was used as a schoolroom for infants, and in 1870 as a girls school. Its use as a school ceased in 1887.

The church and tithes of Basingstoke were given by the Conqueror to the Abbey of Mount St Michael. In 1233 they were purchased by Peter des Roches, Bishop of Winchester, and given to Selborne Priory which in 1464 rebuilt the chancel. Bishop Fox of Winchester rebuilt the tower, nave and aisles in the sixteenth century and he intended to rebuild the chancel

Basingstoke Town Hall

and south chapel. This was not done and the chancel roof of 1464 remains. As a dated roof it is of great value. Attention was drawn to it above when describing the Brethren's Hall at St Cross—both roofs are near in style and date. This roof construction, with side purlins, butted in line between principal rafters and triangulated by windbraces, appears with some frequency in Hampshire.

138

To the north of the town on rising ground the ruins of the Guild chapel of the Holy Trinity and Holy Ghost Chapel seen from the railway station, are in Chapel Hill Cemetery. Little of the Holy Ghost Chapel remains: the ruins are mostly of the chapel of the Holy Trinity built in 1524 by Lord Sandys of the Vyne, of brick faced with stone in a decorative late Gothic style to house the tombs of his family.

The cemetery or 'liten' was established outside the town during the reign of King John in 1204 when churchyards were closed, but later the ground was consecrated and the Holy Ghost Chapel was erected at least by the early thirteenth century. The Fraternity of the Guild of the Holy Ghost, established by 1480 and re-established by a charter confirming its legality, not its foundation, by Henry VIII in 1524, was not suppressed under the Act of 1545 because of the king's death, but dissolved by Edward VI in 1547. It was refounded in 1557 under Mary I for the education of boys, the school being conducted in a schoolroom built in the remains of the Holy Trinity Chapel—the place where Gilbert White of Selborne began his education.

The Holy Ghost Chapel, Chapel Hill, Basingstoke

The school continued until 1855 when the old schoolroom was pulled down and with the new title of the Queen's Free School moved to new premises in Salisbury Road. The use of the land adjoining the Holy Ghost Chapel for burials and 'a playground for the children of the town' ceased in 1856. Part of the old town survives to the south and ancient streets—Church Street and Wote Street—lead to the old Market Square at the centre, graced by the handsome Town Hall of 1832, a successor to the Mote Hall—which might have given its name to Wote Street. It is recorded that in 1832 the Town Hall was 'a large room supported on pillars' then in 1865 'the open space was enclosed' and in 1887 'a clocktower was added in honour of the Jubilee'. The clocktower, shown in photographs of the period, has been removed. The old Corn Exchange built in 1865 is in Wote Street and is now the Haymarket Theatre.

The main streets, Winchester Street and London Street—the latter now closed to traffic—have many good buildings. The National Westminster Bank is a stock brick Italianate building of 1864, there is an impressive congregational church of 1860 with a large Tuscan portico, and at the end of London Street are the Deane Almshouses, founded in 1607 by Sir James Deane to accommodate six widows of Basingstoke and two of Deane.

The District Council offices east of New Road, which complete the eastern end of the town, are in a restored eighteenth-century brick house, surrounded by pleasant gardens. Once one of the great mansions of Hampshire and less than two miles from Basingstoke Parish Church, Basing House developed from defensive works built by Hugh de Port in the twelfth century which took the form of a fortified keep on a motte defended by an encircling upper wall. In plan it was similar to Ludgershall and Old Sarum. Basing passed by marriage to the Paulets in 1428, and Sir William Paulet, Marquis of Winchester, built a large brick mansion on the castle site in the mid-1500s. The twelfth-century work was removed except for a few flint foundations and the motte was covered with buildings. This was the Old House—the New House, built nearby, followed at a later date. Basing House thus became a vast complex and one of the finest brick Tudor mansions of its time.

During the Civil War Sir John Paulet declared for the king but later hoped to placate Cromwell by complying with a request in 1641 to sell his armoury and thereby 'preserved his quiet'. However, this was not to be: the house was too strategically placed to be allowed to remain in Royalist hands and Cromwell ordered its surrender. At first the party remaining in the house defended

Haymarket Theatre, Basingstoke

themselves successfully and beat off all attacks, but Cromwell himself took command and brought in Dutch cannon. The final stages of the fighting in October 1645 were vicious and the surrender of the garrison ignominious.

The Marquis was imprisoned in the Tower but later allowed to go to France. Several priests were executed on the spot and about two hundred prisoners taken, including seventy-years-old Inigo Jones, the architect, who was robbed of his clothes and brought out in a blanket. The total value of the plunder was said to have been two hundred thousand pounds. Cromwell ordered total demolition of the house and many houses in

141

Basing were built with, or contain, bricks from the ruins which for many years were used as a 'quarry'. For example, a bridge over the Basingstoke Canal was built with them. The site is dramatic. On the massive motte and surrounding area the scattered excavated ruins trace out the plan of the house. Part of a gatehouse on the north side survives, and near the Basingstoke Canal a pigeon-house in which pigeons were bred for the cooking pot contains a potence in working order. The site is administered by Hampshire County Council and is open to the public.

The pigeon-house at Basing House

Grange Farm is seventeenth century. It has a charming small granary, also known as the 'tithe barn', a massive barn of brick laid in English bond that could pre-date the siege. It has two wagon entrances with small openings to the south, buttressed walls in superb brickwork and an elegant roof with two tiers of butted side purlins with curved wind braces. The lower collars are slightly cambered and supported by arched braces. They each support four queen struts, two of which extend to upper collars above which are 'V' struts.

A Norman church with central tower and transepts, which probably had subsequent alterations and additions, was rebuilt in brick with stone facings by the Paulets in the sixteenth century. Sections of the north and south arches of the tower, and a re-used thirteenth-century doorway in the north aisle, are all that remains of work earlier than 1519. The church has a nave and aisles of equal length with a central tower and a chancel with north and south chapels. The nave, aisles and tower are of 1519, the north chapel is of 1525 and the south chapel dates from 1543. The size of the church and the high quality of the architecture can be appreciated from the south-west, but for beauty of a special kind I never tire of the exterior east end, where the gabled north and south chapels and chancel, each with large windows all different, are of approximately equal size and combine with the tower to produce a majestic composition made delectable by a variety of textures formed by brick, flint, stone, and plaster, all beautifully mellowed by time. The fine roofs of the nave and aisles survive from 1519, the principal rafters have scissor braces and there are two tiers of butted purlins with curved wind braces.

Daneshill, to the north-west, was built by Edwin Lutyens who used local bricks from a brickyard started by Walter Hoare, who found that the earth there recaptured the quality of Tudor bricks. Lutyens designed special moulded shapes for him and used them for fireplaces—the forerunners, alas, of 'brickette' fireplaces.

To the north of Basingstoke, The Vyne at Sherborne St John is an important house, built of brick between 1518 and 1527 by William Sandys, created Lord Sandys of The Vyne by Henry VIII in 1523, and made Lord Chamberlain in 1526. A place of great charm where architecture and setting enhance each other, Lord Sandys' house, like that of another of Henry's favourites, Sutton Place in Surrey, appears to have an unusual plan for its date. However, like Sutton Place alterations have been made and the sixteenth-century arrangement of the principal rooms can only be identified from an inventory made in 1541 by Lord Sandys' widow. Believed to have had a base court to the north the plan is now E-shaped, formed by the central block and two wings. The central porch is seventeenth century and replaces an original one. The centre block is two rooms deep with a 'great dining chamber' and withdrawing-rooms.

A long gallery which occupies the whole first floor of the west wing has original linen fold panelling dated by the devices of two notable personalities carved upon it. It cannot date before 1522, when Tunstall became Bishop of London, and not later than 1528 when Wolsey was disgraced.

The Vyne, Basingstoke, built by Lord Sandys, 1518-27

The high quality of this gallery is equalled by the chapel, which is an eastward extension built to incorporate foundations of a former chapel of the Virgin. Built of brick comparable with Lord Sandys' Holy Trinity Chapel of 1524 at Basingstoke, it could be of a similar date. Inside are original stalls beneath a canopy which curves forward over carved and traceried backs and panelled fronts, and poppy heads terminate the stall ends. The stained glass in the chapel is early sixteenth-century Flemish work, brought from the chapel of the Holy Ghost, Basingstoke.

In 1653 The Vyne was purchased by Chaloner Chute from the son of Colonel Sandys, who fell at the Battle of Cheriton in 1644. Chaloner Chute was elected Speaker of the House of Commons in 1659 during Richard Cromwell's Parliament, because he 'entertained hope of being able to serve the King'. Around 1655 he employed John Webb to make various additions and alterations at The Vyne, such as providing new fireplaces: also removing tracery from window openings—the cost, fourteen shillings each, is documented. Webb's principal contribution was the large stuccoed brick and wooden portico on the north front, one of the earliest of its kind in England and influenced by his uncle, Inigo Jones. Jones, in turn, was influenced by Palladio's work in the Veneto. The Venetian window in Quarley church marked the acceptance of Palladian principles by 1725—the portico at The Vyne was pioneer work following the Civil War.

By 1754 The Vyne passed to John Chute, who was praised by Walpole as 'an exquisite architect of the purest taste'. If he designed the quite splendid principal staircase then this was so. John Chute built the Tomb Room, to the south-east of the old Tudor Chapel, as a memorial to Chaloner Chute. The monument is by Thomas Carter of Piccadilly, London, where he made chimney-pieces for large houses of the time and worked from designs by Robert Adam, James Stuart, and others. His price

A garden pavilion at The Vyne, by John Webb

145

was £260 for the drawing-room fireplace in Croome Court. At The Vyne he worked under the guidance of John Chute, and the effigy of Chaloner Chute is exceptional in its quality. The sarcophagus is superb, and most likely attributable to the designing skill of John Chute, although he died in 1776 shortly before the work was completed. Bills have survived—the cost of the marble in November 1775 was £186.7½d. The Vyne is a National Trust Property and open to the public.

In the wooded countryside near The Vyne are the Sherbornes, Pamber and Bramley, all villages on lands once held by the powerful Hugh de Port following the Conquest. Subsequently the Paulet St John family held lands in the area—hence Sherborne St John, where there is a much-restored church with a delightful brick porch, dated 1533, and inside, over the doorway into the church the kneeling figures of the donors James Spier and his wife. Good stained glass in the north aisle shows the influence of the Renaissance. Monk Sherborne church has an impressive porch with two massive, shaped timbers which together form the entrance opening. Early Norman work remains, including herring-bone flint work. An eastern arch suggests that the chancel had an apse.

Pamber church as it is known locally, serves as a parish church, but it was originally the church of the priory of Monk Sherborne, founded by Hugh de Port as a Benedictine cell of Cerisy-la-Forêt. As an alien priory, it fell under suspicion of aiding the enemy in the French wars and was suppressed by Henry V in 1414. In 1462 Edward IV gave its property to God's House, Southampton. It eventually passed to Queen's College, Oxford. Dedicated by Bishop Giffard in the early twelfth century, building continued and the long presbytery was completed by the early thirteenth century. This with the tower forms the present church. Three lancet windows at the east end splayed inside have a keeled edge roll with moulded bases but without capitals. A mid-thirteenth-century wooden effigy of an unknown knight, skilfully carved and detailed, lies in a western recess in the south wall. Traces of paint remain. In its sylvan setting the priory is picturesque—and melancholy too—for it recalls the power and wealth of a religion long gone.

Bramley, the northern village of this group, has a timber-framed manor house in which the wealth of its builder is proclaimed by an extravagant use of timber which is more decorative than structural.

Bramley church nearby is of interest for the chancel screen. It is the lower part of a rood loft set up in 1525, and surviving

Pamber Priory, north-east Hampshire

churchwarden accounts record that alabaster images were purchased and placed in position in 1533, but had to be pulled down in 1547 under the Act of Edward VI. It has been suggested that its extent and position is indicated by panelling in the roof above—a canopy of grace—which is lit by a window in the roof on the north side. This should be compared with a similar arrangement at Greywell which is without doubt a genuine survival of the early sixteenth century. Mention should be made of Soane's south chapel, built in 1801 to house an impressive

147

marble effigy by Thomas Carter of Bernard Brocas, who died in 1777. It is comparable with Carter's effigy of Chaloner Chute at The Vyne for high quality carving and portrayal of character.

Unlike many other Roman towns in Britain, which at least survive as an influence on the plan of a subsequent town, Roman Silchester had no such successor. Large sections of its walls alone survive above ground. The site was excavated in the late nineteenth century (1864-1909) and the network of roads, defensive works and the siting of buildings—including the earliest Christian temple in Britain—were recorded before being re-covered with earth. However, excavation continues and a museum on the site should be visited, together with the exhibits in Reading Museum, deposited by the Duke of Wellington.

Silchester church stands on the east side of the Roman town site just within the flint walls and a cottage named The Mount, to the north of the church, had an open hall and is of cruck construction with a later bay added.

A grateful nation presented the Duke of Wellington with a country estate as a reward for ridding them of a European tyrant. The victor of Waterloo was certainly a little more modest in his choice than the Duke of Marlborough, earlier so rewarded for his victory at Blenheim: he chose Stratfield Saye, for the existing mansion interested him far less than the good and profitable farms on the estate. He had intended to rebuild on higher ground above the old mansion anyway, and had collected various architectural items on his travels for the purpose— but the new house did not materialize.

Stratfield Saye house is of brick, two storeys high, built by Sir William Pitt—relative of Thomas Pitt of Abbotts Ann—in the mid-seventeenth century. George Pitt, the first Lord Rivers, made additions and improvements in the late eighteenth century, including a long gallery, dining-room, library and other rooms. He also raised the height of the hall by removing the rooms above it. The first Duke of Wellington added the porch in 1838 and raised the height of the wings. Although much altered, the character of the seventeenth-century brick house remains. Large Dutch gables terminate the wings and pilasters with a small pediment add distinction to the façade. The well-designed cupola is modern. Open to the public, the house contains many treasures associated with the first duke. Wellington Country Park three miles away provides a variety of attractions for an interesting day out.

The small church in the grounds was built and probably designed by Lord Rivers in 1754-8, to replace the old church near the house. Classical churches, in rural situations, certainly seem to acquire a damp melancholy air and architecturally they are an acquired taste. The preference for Gothic dies hard and the little church of Stratfield Saye has some critics, most often being diplomatically described as 'interesting'. I admire it immensely.

There is a delightful early nineteenth-century rectory near the church, it has a porch with four Tuscan columns and a lunette window above. Classical motifs are acceptable when applied to domestic architecture!

Much favoured—in the past at least—by the oak tree, this area has several important timber-framed buildings; not only barns and houses, but churches also. Hartley Wespall is one of a group of three within a few miles of each other—the other two are Rotherwick to the south-east and Mattingley church to the east.

Hartley Wespall, the oldest of this group, was restored by George Gilbert Scott Junior and some quite breathtaking original timber-framing to be seen externally in the west wall of the nave is but a prelude to a greater wealth of timbering within.

The nave of three bays has cambered tie-beams with wide arched braces upon principal posts with a well undercut roll moulding. A crown post stands upon each tie-beam to support a centre purlin passing beneath cambered collars. Struts pass from each crown post upwards to the collars and the purlin.

The appearance of an early crown-post roof in Hampshire is noteworthy. This particular roof has been dated to c. 1330 by the *Victoria Country History*—might one suppose that it was erected before side purlin construction came into local use? A possible reason for the distinctive character of this building is that the manor was held by the Bishops of Bath and Wells during the early fourteenth century—the cusping on the massive braces in the west end of the nave would alone suggest west country influence.

A very delicate, and obviously accurate, pencil drawing made of the church before its restoration is preserved. It shows a small timber-framed tower with a spire at the west end of the nave—the tower must have been similar to the tower at Yateley but much smaller. Scott removed the west tower in 1868 and added the present one on the north-east. Dr Keate, the flogging headmaster of Eton, was rector here at the time of Scott's restoration and lies buried in the chancel.

Rotherwick church, three miles south of Hartley Wespall, no longer has its original timber-framed walls. These, except for

The Roman wall, Silchester

short lengths of the principal posts, were replaced—or remain encased in sixteenth-century brickwork much of which is in a random bond, with sections in English bond. The timber roof of the old nave survives. It has scissor braces with two tiers of butted side purlins and wind braces similar to the roofs of Old Basing church. The west tower, dated seventeenth century, is also of brick, but in Flemish bond. The house to the west of the church may well have been the priest's house.

At Mattingley church, three miles north-east of Rotherwick, there is a lavish use of timber—especially externally in the Victorian aisles, in which there is close studding with herring-bone brickwork infill. Softwood was chosen for much of the internal Victorian work, and was even used to make up the outer sides of the original oak arcade posts. Arched braces pass longitudinally beneath the arcade plates, and cambered tie-beams have curved braces with a moulding which is continuous across their span and down the arcade posts. There is an arch-braced collar beam above and a single row of through side purlins on each side have curved wind braces. The Victorian aisle roofs are continuous with the nave roof. The exterior of this building is spoilt by the Victorian aisles, but the interior of the nave and chancel is superb.

Neville Chamberlain, Prime Minister at the commencement of Hitler's war, died of a broken heart in 1940. Deceived by Hitler and then told by his colleagues' In the name of God, go' his last days were spent at Heckfield, a few miles to the north of the A32, in a Georgian house near the church now used as a conference centre. The church was much restored by Butter-field, but its sixteenth-century tower, built with toffee-coloured conglomerate on sarsen stone footings, appears to have escaped over-restoration.

Bramshill Park is to the east of Heckfield, and although a Police College for senior officers and not open to the public it must be mentioned as it is one of the largest houses of its period in the county. It was built in 1605-12 by Edward Lord Zouch of Haringworth, of brick with a minimum of stone dressings, and was planned to give an immediate impression of opulence by concentration upon a quite magnificent front façade.

In the park, not far from the house, an oak tree records the spot where Archbishop George Abbot accidentally shot and killed a forester while stag-hunting. It was a tragic accident and one, it is said, that George Abbot was never allowed to forget.

Eversley is about three miles to the north of Bramshill House and was the home of two men now highly thought of. One, a

Mattingley church: the interior

writer, was Charles Kingsley, the other was John James, an architect. John James, the son of a parson, was associated with architects of Wren's circle. Clerk of the works at Greenwich in 1705 and assistant surveyor at St Paul's in 1711, his best-known building in London, St George's in Hanover Square, was completed in 1724. Eversley church, excluding the chancel, is also believed to have been built of brick by James.

Warbrook House, built by James for himself in 1724, has a delicacy of touch not usually found in the followers of Wren. I first saw the house one morning in spring—the gardens were yellow with daffodils reflected in the ornamental canal. The sight was unforgettable.

Charles Kingsley, author of *The Water Babies* and other works, went to Eversley as curate for a time in 1842, and was recalled in 1844 to be rector. He loved the place and remained there until his death in 1875, but said that the population was mostly composed of 'heth croppers'—poachers by instinct and heritage. The countryside is north of the chalk upland, and in places, poor heathland with pinewoods.

153

Kingsley is buried in Eversley churchyard near an avenue of Irish yew trees planted by him. They lead to the church porch, which with the nave, was rebuilt in brick by John James in 1724. The tower, also of brick, was completed in 1735. A chancel screen erected at this time is claimed to be the only eighteenth-century chancel screen in Hampshire, but when the chancel was altered in 1873 it was changed and repainted with Victorian decoration—the lilies on the eastern panels are believed to have been designed by Charles Kingsley.

A large sarsen stone below the floor of the north aisle may be seen beneath a trap-door. Yellow-brown in colour and always damp, it may be part of the foundations of a heathen place of worship. I find it repulsive and sinister.

On 5 May 1979 fire destroyed Yateley church leaving only the walls, the porch and the tower. The church was rebuilt and consecrated on 21 November 1981—a remarkable achievement which has been recorded in a well-produced commemorative booklet.

The north nave wall contains eleventh-century work with long and short quoins, plastered over in 1952, and also a blocked window, but the most interesting feature is the timber-framed west tower built in the fifteenth century. A shingled bell-tower is carried on posts and has 'aisles' to the north, south and west which are close studded and infilled with modern brick. The tower required extensive repairs following the fire.

After Sedan, Napoleon III, the Empress and the Prince Imperial took refuge at Chislehurst in Kent where the Emperor died in 1873. The Prince was killed in the Zulu War six years later, and the saddened Empress bought Farnborough Hill at Farnborough and lived there until her death in 1920 aged ninety-four. The house is now a school.

Nearby, off the A325 and near to the Woking-Basingstoke railway is the Benedictine Abbey of St Michael, built by the Empress in 1886 to serve the chapel above a mausoleum containing the sarcophagi of Napoleon III and the Prince Imperial, presented by Queen Victoria. It also contains the sarcophagus of the Empress.

Impressive abbey buildings in a pleasant wooded setting are of brick and stone in a Romanesque style while the chapel by Distailleur, which stands apart on rising ground surrounded by trees is in the French Flamboyant style—a magnificent building. Visitors are conducted into the mausoleum on Wednesdays and Saturdays at three o'clock and on Sundays at four o'clock.

To the west near Hartley Wintney is Elvetham Hall, an

immense Victorian mansion built by S.S. Teulon in 1860 for Lord Calthorpe. It replaces a former house visited in 1591 by Elizabeth I as a guest of the Earl of Hertford, who in two weeks spent a fortune on her entertainment. He even constructed a lake especially for the occasion, traces of which are still visible, and contrived a series of water pageants and naval displays. The present house and park is a conference centre and not open to the public.

West Green House, an attractive National Trust property, stands south-east of Mattingley. A small house of brick damaged by fire, it is now repaired and contains work of several periods from the early to the late eighteenth century. The west front has a central door with a heavy rusticated surround and circular niches with busts occupying the first-floor level.

Winchfield to the south-east has a remarkable Norman church in which the detail is somewhat bold to say the least. Restored by Woodyer in 1850, it is difficult to be sure which is re-tooled original and which is entirely Woodyer. The chancel arch is perhaps the show-piece and displays a full array of Norman work (or Victorian Norman style) gone mad—but well worth seeing.

Dogmersfield to the south-east like Elvetham is a large park with a history extending to pre-Reformation times. The Bishops of Bath and Wells held the manor and Henry VIII often visited their palace where, with Prince Arthur, he met Catherine of Aragon. After the Dissolution of the Monasteries Henry VIII's Lord Chancellor, Thomas Wriothesley, first Earl of Southampton, acquired the manor by being in the right place at the right time, just as he had gained ownership of Titchfield Abbey and much more. The second Earl built a house in the park and the brick pigeon house in the driveway may date to his time.

The present house, which became Dogmersfield College, was built by Martha Goodyer and her husband Ellis St John in 1728. Their son, Henry, enlarged the house and landscaped the park, removing the village in the process and making a lake. The grottoes and follies have all gone save one, the 'King John's Hunting Lodge', but the map shows how Sir Henry forced the builders of the Basingstoke Canal to make a detour around his park.

The old parish church in the park near the house was demolished—a new one built near the drive to the house in 1806 is of brick with a battlemented tower and two-bay nave, but no chancel. Abandoned after another church was built in a more convenient position at the small settlement of Pilcott, it has

155

recently been turned into a very unusual private residence.

North Warnborough, to the south-west of Dogmersfield Park in the parish of Odiham, has many pleasant cottages, several of which are of interest. Thatched Cottage is of cruck construction with three bays and probably conformed to the usual arrangement of a central open hall and floored end bays, one containing service rooms, the other a parlour. Reputed to be fifteenth century, it is more likely to be mid-sixteenth.

Thatched Cottage, North Warnbrough—a fine example of cruck construction

Odiham Castle, built by King John, is a picturesque ruin of flint near the Basingstoke Canal which has the only octagonal keep in England. It was frequently visited by King John, who resided there in June 1215 before leaving for Runnymede to sign the Magna Carta: he later returned on his way to Winchester. In recent years there have been various suggestions for its use, but it is now in the care of Hampshire County Council and will presumably be preserved as a ruin. Unfortunately buildings of flint make rather untidy ruins.

Greywell, westwards along the canal from Odiham Castle, is near the entrance to the three-quarter mile canal tunnel built in 1792 to avoid winding around a private estate before reaching Basingstoke. There was no towpath within the tunnel, so bargees had to 'leg it' by pushing with their feet against the sides or the roof. A roof collapse in 1872 put the tunnel out of use and the canal ends at Greywell.

After a period of neglect voluntary labour has come forward with great enthusiasm to make the waterway navigable again with the intention of opening it from Greywell through Byfleet to the Thames at Weybridge. It is now under the auspices of the Surrey and Hampshire County Councils.

A liberal use of timber in the construction of many old houses at Greywell reflects the wealth of woodland in the district, and the small church a short distance from the main road down a pathway is important for the remarkable survival of a rood screen and loft which has a stair turret projecting from the north wall of the nave.

St Swithun's Church at Nately Scures, a single-cell church of about 1175 with an apsidal east end, is one of the smallest churches in Hampshire. Built of flint with Binstead stone dressings it remains one of only four apsidal single-cell churches in England. Others are at Winterborne Tomson in Dorset, North Marden, Sussex, and Little Tey, Essex. The church is also noted for its north door with semicircular head and zigzag decoration. It has a capital carved with a mermaid holding a plait of her hair.

In contrast to Nately the church at Odiham is large, even oversize. The seventeenth-century west tower flanked by the gables of the aisles is a grand composition of brick laid in English bond with pilasters at the angles and at the belfry openings. The free interpretation of classical motifs in the brickwork of this period is always exciting and ingenious, and Odiham church tower is no exception. At the south-west corner of the church-yard a small pest house, in the process of restoration as I write, was originally used to isolate victims of infectious diseases such as the 'pox'.

Odiham High Street is wide and lined with a variety of build-ings, many timber-framed and much older at the rear than their eighteenth-century brick façades would suggest. The nucleus of the old town is centred around the Bury, a square adjoining the churchyard to the north, and here the stocks and a whipping-post are preserved.

Crondall, near the Surrey boundary, has good brick houses in Church Street, several timber-framed, including The Limes which is of cruck construction. The church is claimed to be the finest in the county. In about 1659 the alarming condition of the Norman central tower made its removal necessary and it was replaced by a brick tower built on the north side of the chancel which was modelled on Battersea church tower. Apart from the tower much of the original twelfth-century Norman church remains, although the repair work and restoration of the seventeenth and nineteenth centuries has left its mark: Victorian 'Norman' work can be misleading—as we found at Winchfield.

10 From Bentley to Langstone Harbour—the Portsmouth Road

South of Crondall on the A31 at Bentley a sign in the form of an open book displaying a map and places of interest in the village was an idea initiated by Lord Baden-Powell, who lived for many years at Pax Hill nearby. Standing on rising ground the church, shown on the sign, has a Norman tower of part eighteenth-century brick. The nave and aisles were entirely rebuilt in the nineteenth century, all the old work being in the early Norman chancel and side chapels, and the clerestory windows above the chancel arcades were added in the fifteenth century. A good example of the use of local building materials, the durability of chalk as a building stone is well demonstrated.

A western arm of the River Wey meandering from tributary streams south of Alton provided power for mills now silent, including Isington Mill, the home, until his death in 1970, of Viscount Montgomery of Alamein, the veteran commander of wartime campaigns in the Western Desert and Europe.

From Isington lanes lead beneath the railway to the Forest of Alice Holt, a remnant of heath and dense woodland notorious in the past for the cover it afforded robbers and highwaymen. It formed part of an almost continuous belt of woodland and un-cultivated heath extending southward along the western edge of the Weald, including the Forests of Woolmer and Liss and also the Forest of Bere which once extended from Farley Mount into Sussex.

Alice Holt provided timber for the re-roofing of Westminster Hall, London, by master carpenter Hugh Herland between 1394 and 1402, who constructed a hammer-beam roof modestly reported by the Royal Commission on Historic Monuments to be 'probably the finest timber-roofed building in Europe'. Framed at Farnham in Surrey before transport to London by road and the Thames, some of the smaller beams are twenty-one feet long with a section of two feet by three.

In the seventeenth and eighteenth centuries the forests were greatly reduced by requirements of Royal Navy ships—one thousand loads were taken from Alice Holt in 1784.

Following excavations in 1958-61 at a site in the Alice Holt forest between Bucks Horn Oak and Frith End, remains of Roman pottery kilns were discovered together with many shards. The pottery, a native coarse ware for local use, was tentatively dated as from the second to the fourth century.

The River Slea and the southern arm of the River Wey drain marshy heathland around the army village of Bordon, south of which at Blackmoor the first Earl of Selborne commissioned Alfred Waterhouse to build a mansion and a church in 1868–73. Developments of this sort on a smaller scale are characteristic of the area, where expensive houses are sited discreetly in woodland.

Bramshott Manor, an important house near Bramshott church dating from the fourteenth century, was a first-floor hall house and has a crown-post roof with painted decoration. Once known as 'Old House', a farmhouse for many years it is now a private residence. The restored thirteenth-century church—'mother' church of Liss and Liphook—has a Victorian broach spire which is very pleasing in its wooded setting. At Bramshott Grange to the south-east, a small sixteenth-century gatehouse of brick belonged to a former house, Bramshott Place, which is now gone; it has four large shaped gables and moulded brick provides much surface detail.

Wakeners Wells a mile north-east of Bramshott church are a series of hammer ponds constructed by the Hooke family in the seventeenth century to provide power for producing iron from ironstone found locally. The abundance of slag heaps in the area and the incidence of names such as Henry atte Cinderheap, together with recorded baptisms of children born to 'strangers at the forge', is further indication of an extensive former iron industry in the area.

Liphook in the parish of Bramshott is not an ancient settlement, but came into being to serve travellers on the Portsmouth Road. Samuel Pepys travelled the road and wrote of the perils experienced—especially the fear of becoming lost—and also of the welcome hospitality to be found at Liphook. He probably rested at The Crown, which was later closed down. The Royal Anchor Inn—formerly the Anchor Inn—became, to quote Sir Albert Richardson, 'A great coaching house with a nautical air'. He dated it about 1745. Many famous personalities were entertained here, including Lord Nelson, Marshal von Blücher and members of royalty—the Duchess of Kent rested for a night at the inn with her daughter who later became Queen Victoria.

Petersfield had the advantage of being the oldest borough in the county after Southampton, Stockbridge and Winchester, and in the twelfth century the Lord of the Manor, the Earl of Gloucester, granted the burgesses all the rights enjoyed by the citizens of Winchester with a right to have a merchant guild.

With changes from arable to sheep farming in the fourteenth century, the town prospered as a wool market with continental buyers arriving to purchase the fine quality Downland wool, as well as cloth and later leather. The town benefited from its position on the Portsmouth Road especially in the early nineteenth century when nearly thirty coaches a day passed through, until the railway arrived in the 1850s and the trade fell away.

The character of The Square is enhanced by a fine equestrian statue of William III. Made in lead and originally gilded, it is probably by John Cheere, who at his yard near the Green Park,

The statue of William III, at Petersfield

London produced a great quantity of works mostly of lead—statues and busts of shepherdesses and haymakers for gardens, Roman soldiers and many more. The statue stood in the grounds of Petersfield House near the church, home of Sir William Jolliffe and given to the town when the house was demolished in 1793. Ridiculed by many, this excellent work in the fashion of its time is interesting to horsemen as it depicts—with not a little artist's licence—a type of horse—cross-breed of barb with Arab, a powerful but agile animal bred for cavalry. The nearest to the type now bred is ridden in dressage work—the Lipizzaner.

A variety of buildings, some eighteenth century, together with the church provide a pleasant country market town atmosphere. This is especially true of the houses in the south-west corner of The Square, which have a pleasant Georgian air, and nearby High Street is lined with several fine houses of red brick, particularly numbers twenty, twenty-one and twenty-two. Number eighteen, with a grand Roman Doric porch regrettably stuccoed with a textured surface, stands opposite a stuccoed framed building with a gable, dated 1613. Now a shop, it has an early eighteenth-century hood over a doorway. In College Street the Red Lion Hotel of brick has a pediment and handsome doorway flanked by Roman Doric columns. At the north end of the street are Antrobus Almshouses (1622), and opposite Churcher's College, built of blue and red brick chequer in 1729 and founded by the will of a wealthy East Indies merchant, Richard Churcher.

The school prepared boys to become apprentices to masters of ships making their voyages to the East Indies, but with aims unsuited to the town the school became a Blue Coat school in 1744 offering ordinary education. Satisfactory education, however, was not obtained until the Endowed Schools and Charity Commissioners intervened. The college, now situated at the top of Remshill, moved in 1881. Professor Stuart Piggot the eminent archaeologist was a scholar here.

From the south-west corner of The Square, Sheep Street leads past nineteenth-century cottages and a continuous jettied row of dwellings to The Spain, so-called it is believed, after the foreign merchants who traded there for wool and cloth. It is a quiet area, with a green bordered by handsome Georgian houses and also Tulley's, externally modern in appearance but part of a wealden house, of which the hall and one bay survives. John Goodyer, the botanist who lived nearby in a house identified by a plaque, pioneered later work by Linnaeus and Gilbert White and was so highly thought of in his time that even, during the turmoil of the Civil War, Lord Hopton, who garrisoned the town, ordered that he be protected 'from all dangers, damages, disturbances and oppressions whatsoever'.

The early twelfth-century church on the south side of The Square contains some of the finest Norman work in the county. Built on a cruciform plan with the unusual addition of a west tower, aisles the width of the transepts were added to the nave at the end of the twelfth century when the nave arcades of four bays were constructed. The central tower may not have been finished, or may have suffered damage—there is evidence of a fire—and its west wall has been taken down. However the former east arch became the chancel arch and the three windows above decorated with shafting and zigzag mouldings, together with a third window in the gable, were opened to the nave. Restoration in 1874 by Sir Arthur Blomfield was extensive and included the addition of the clerestory windows and much neo-Norman work in the nave and elsewhere.

The Heath is a large public recreation ground to the east of the town which was formed in 1867 with a lake more than twenty acres in extent resulting from drainage work in the eighteenth century. It is possibly as popular now as in the nineteenth century, when volunteer bands delighted audiences on Music Hill. Also on The Heath is a large Bronze Age necropolis of twenty-one barrows.

The Queen Elizabeth Park south of Petersfield, with magnificent views from Downland walks, includes Butser Hill, the highest point in Hampshire. It also provides an excellent site for the Ancient Farm Research Project, a working farmstead where knowledge obtained from excavation concerning farming methods of around 3000 BC is tested by growing crops and rearing animals under controlled conditions. Dexter cows and Soay sheep approximating to prehistoric breeds have been introduced and round huts built with the aid of evidence gained from Maiden Castle and Balksbury. Experiments with pottery are also conducted. The park is open all the year round, other attractions including craft demonstrations, a bookshop, a film theatre and a cafe. There is a small parking fee only.

The family home of Edward Gibbon, author of *The History of the Decline and Fall of the Roman Empire,* was at Buriton, east of the A3 under Head Down. His father bought the Manor House near the church, a building of which he wrote, 'It has been converted into the fashion and convenience of a modern house'. Gibbon was personally abused by those who thought his book challenged established religious belief but criticism turned to praise

and critics described his book as, 'the one English history which may be regarded as definitive'. The first volume was published when he was thirty-nine, the last at forty-six. He recalled that in 1764 the idea of writing the history 'first started in my mind musing amidst the ruins of the Capitol, where bare-foot friars were singing vespers ing the Temple of Jupiter'.

Lanes from Buriton lead southward across downland to Chalton, a small village with a medieval public house and a church of distinction facing each other across an irregular

The south-west corner of The Square, Petersfield

sloping green. The public house, named the Red Lion, is a wealden house and one of the best examples of its kind in Hampshire. The church has an elegant Early English chancel with long lancets, a four-light geometrical east window and a double piscina. A south transeptal chapel containing the font has a two-light south window. Possibly dating from the four-teenth century, it is a lovely feature—especially on a sunny day when light floods in through the window.

Eastwards over Chalton Down there is a wide valley running

165

southward where the small isolated St Hubert's Chapel at Idsworth stands in fields on the valley side. The manor house has gone, abandoned when the railway came; stables—now a cottage—and an avenue of lime trees remain. Also in the fields near the chapel may be seen raised platforms indicating the positions of buildings in the vanished medieval village.

Claims that the chapel was built by Earl Godwin, father of King Harold, rest upon the evidence of a round-headed window and a blocked doorway in the north wall. The nave is stated to be twelfth century, widened to the south in the sixteenth century. It has an Early English chancel. Neglected until 1912, Victorian restoration was avoided and H.S. Goodhart-Rendel repaired the chapel with care. A seventeenth-century pulpit and other fittings were kept, new work carefully introduced where necessary.

Paintings on the north wall of the chancel date from the early fourteenth century and depict a hunting scene taken from the life of St Hubert with the curing of a man who believes himself to be a wolf. Separated by a horizontal border the story of St John the Baptist is also illustrated showing Salome dancing.

St Hubert's Chapel, Idsworth

Wall-paintings of a similar period exist in several Hampshire churches, survivors of many destroyed by iconoclasts and church restorers rather than by natural decay. All churches possessed mural paintings, and the fragments in our churches belonged to a series of related paintings covering the walls.

In my own experience the paintings in the small churches of Crete offer a good parallel. The effect of such interiors to receptive modern eyes is one of breathtaking wonder, the viewer not necessarily awed by any identifiable religious content but by the jewel-like decoration and lively portrayal of figures in another world, as if one had entered a jewel-box. Those for whom the paintings were intended found different cause for wonder. Devotional and instructive themes included Bible stories and the virtuous lives and figures of saints who, as in the Orthodox Church, may have been worshipped, cajoled and blamed in effigy as if physically present. Moralities gave an unlettered congregation graphic illustration of the rewards of virtue, but fearful damnation was the reward of sin.

Meaning was conveyed by a symbolism understood by all. Gestures of the body, the clothes worn and the attributes were part of a universal language.

Technical skill varied, but established styles were slow to change. Expressive rapid drawing in line with a brush characterized English painting, areas of flat colour innocent of chiaroscuro were added. The limitation of colours available blessed the artist for he could not avoid producing a harmonious colour scheme based on yellow ochre with other brown and red earth colours modified with carbon black.

Paintings on plaster walls depend upon the adhesion of colours by the chemical change of calcium hydrate to calcium carbonate by taking up carbon dioxide in the drying process.

Buon fresco is the term applied to a technique in which the pigment, ground and tempered with limewater, is applied to wet fresh plaster only. Of necessity the work has to proceed piecemeal. This was the method used by Michelangelo for the Sistine Chapel ceiling.

Secco painting is executed on an established plaster wall roughened and re-wetted with limewater, the pigment ground and tempered with limewater. Sufficient calcium carbonate may remain to provide adhesion of the pigments. However, medieval writers recommended that skimmed milk (casein), egg, or even size made from boiled parchment or leather cuttings could be used to temper the colours; skimmed milk might have been the most frequent choice. Animal fat and drying-oil were avoided.

Both these methods were used. The Sussex group of paintings at Clayton, Hardham, Plumpton and Coombes are buon fresco and the restorer states that early twelfth-century paintings at Witley in Surrey were executed in this manner. However I believe the secco method to have been the most common.

Noxious modern vapours bring rapid destruction and the action of damp is insidious causing slow decay—unfortunately medieval painters in Britain did not insist on cavity walls!

The Bat and Ball Inn westward from the A3 through Cranfield overlooks Broadhalfpenny Down where the Hambledon Cricket Club played and where the laws of cricket were formulated. The Hambledon club did not invent the game but was rather the parent of the Marylebone Club and Broadhalfpenny Down the birthplace of the game known today. The 1770s was the club's finest period: in 1777 they played All England in a match for one thousand guineas and won by an innings and 168 runs. They moved to Windmill Down in 1782, but a stone pillar erected in 1908 on Broadhalfpenny Down near the Bat and Ball Inn records that cricket was played there from 1750-87.

The Bat and Ball, Broadhalfpenny Down, Hambledon

In Hambledon village two miles away, opposite the post office and village shop, a street leading to the church is lined with small houses—many timber-framed, others of Georgian brick and one house a wealden, faced with brick, and the butcher's shop is a charming survival.

Hambledon Manor was held by the Old Minster at Winchester before the Conquest, then by the Bishops of Winchester after 1160. A weekly market and two fairs a year were granted.

Fire destroyed much of the eastern side of the village about

1725, when rebuilding in brick took place; elsewhere several framed houses were concealed by brick fronts. Manor Farm, west of the centre and formerly the manor house, is a thirteenth-century building of stone including a section thought to have been a first-floor domestic chapel. The Victorian west façade conceals a Tudor timber-framed wing.

The parish church sited on the lower slopes of Windmill Hill above the village has a complicated architectural history. Externally it appears to be medieval, with a west tower, an aisled nave and a chancel without aisles. However, it encloses the north and south walls of a pre-Conquest church. To the nave of this church, variously dated from 957-1066, aisles of two bays were added about 1160, first to the north and then followed by the south, semicircular arches with dogtooth and rosette ornament being pierced in the Saxon walls. The west wall of the Saxon church was lost when the thirteenth-century west tower was added. Enlargement of the Saxon chancel arch followed, a pointed arch was inserted and the Saxon wall above retained, dividing the church. Aisles were added to the Saxon chancel, followed by the removal of the Saxon east wall and an extension made eastward. The present long chancel followed.

A vestry added as a western extension of the south aisle formerly had an upper floor connected by a wooden gallery to a similar chamber above the porch. Both date from the fifteenth century and the upper rooms probably provided living accommodation.

A Saxon pilaster strip may be seen above each of the twelfth-century arches pierced in the Saxon nave. A string course—as an eaves course—remains in the north and south walls of the Saxon chancel, that on the south being shorter, part having been lost when a section of wall collapsed during restoration in 1876.

The urban spread from Portsmouth extends along the A3 northward beyond Waterlooville—early nineteenth century in origin as the name suggests—but south-east on the A27 Chichester Road a pleasant oasis is to be found at Bedhampton. The church, still charming, has been restored and the interior whitened, but several eighteenth century and earlier houses remain in pleasant gardens. The Elms is the most outstanding— a seventeenth-century house overlaid in the following century with stucco Gothic detail. An early nineteenth-century owner Sir Theophilus Lee, a Deputy Lieutenant of the County, re-modelled the interior to create the Waterloo Room in a more conventional Classical style in which to entertain the first Duke

Hambledon church

of Wellington. The property is now owned by The Manor Trust, a charitable trust with the object of enhancing the environment and caring for the retired.

While at Bedhampton in January 1819 Keats completed 'The Eve of St Agnes' and in May of the same year wrote 'Ode to a Nightingale' in a Hampstead garden. The glorious year was completed in September with 'Ode to Autumn' written in a house in Great Minster Street, Winchester.

In the pleasant small town of Havant a large church stands at the centre where four roads meet. The exterior of the church is impressive but the nave and tower are Victorian rebuilt in a thirteenth-century style, the nave having been mutilated in 1832 to insert galleries, the tower suffering structural damage as a result. The transepts built in the fifteenth century have west aisles—an unusual feature. The thirteenth-century chancel did not escape mutilation but it has a beautiful quadripartite vault with moulded ribs and bosses. A vestry dating to the fourteenth century, possibly with an upper room, is comparable to the vestry at Hambledon previously mentioned.

Buildings of interest in the town lie at the centre. The only timber-framed house, The Old House at Home, stands near the churchyard in South Street where Georgian brick houses (especially a stock brick house with a large porch and handsome bays) now offices, are to be found. More Georgian houses in East Street, in particular Magnolia House, are of grey and red brick and of interest. The Pallant—still pleasant—can claim one of the finest brick buildings in the town: the Congregational church dated 1718, which is well enough treated, but it is a pity to see it adapted to commercial use.

Warblington signposted from a roundabout on the A27, is situated on a rural coastal strip bordering Langstone Harbour. The village now gone, a church and a ruined castle remain, the centre of population having moved to Emsworth two miles away. The ruins of Warblington Castle may be seen shortly after leaving the main road, the shattered tower of its gatehouse standing above the flat fields. A fortified manor house built between 1514 and 1526 by Margaret Pole, Countess of Salisbury on the site of an earlier house, it changed hands a number of times during the Civil War and was later dismantled. The tower is private property and cannot be visited without permission. Margaret Pole a Plantagenet created Countess of Salisbury by Henry VIII and governess to his daughter Mary Tudor, refused to acknowledge Anne Boleyn as Queen. Her position, and that of her friends, became serious when Cardinal Reginald Pole—

The Elms, Bedhampton, an early house with an eighteenth-century stuccoed front

171

The Old House at Home, a continuous jetty house built in the late sixteenth century

one of her four sons—wrote a book from the safety of Italy condemning Henry's actions against the Roman Church. Afraid of rivalry for the accession from Margaret Pole and her family, Henry had them all executed for treason. Margaret Pole, aged sixty-nine, was executed on Smithfield Green in the precincts

The ruins of Warblington Castle

of the Tower of London on 27 May 1541. The executioner was clumsy and hideously hacked her—it was a bloody and vicious act. The chantry she had prepared at Christchurch Priory remains empty—her body lies in St Peter-ad-Vincula in the Tower of London.

Warblington church evolved from a Saxon predecessor of

173

which only the second storey of a western tower—or porch—remains. In the thirteenth century a nave was constructed west of the Saxon tower. To this aisles were added, terminating level with the eastern face of the tower, the lower stage of which was removed and replaced with pointed chancel arches. The construction of a long chancel followed.

The purpose of the contemporary doorways to be found in the extant section of the Saxon tower—on the north and south faces, together with a blocked doorway on the west face to be seen from within the church—gives rise to speculation. It has been suggested that they gave access to timber platforms, perhaps for the purposes of defence, or simply to give access to the upper stages by ladder avoiding the necessity of building an inside stair.

Described as archaic Early English, the thirteenth-century south nave arcade, a little later than the north, has exceptionally fine piers with detached Purbeck marble shafts and stiff-leaf capitals. A fourteenth-century canopied recess, perhaps used for the reserved sacrament, is to be found in the thirteenth-century north vestry.

Still remote, the presence of two early nineteenth-century watcher's huts of flint and brick in the churchyard recall the gruesome activities of body snatchers and the need to protect this isolated graveyard at that time.

Emsworth in the parish of Warblington stands on the county border with Sussex. It has no medieval church, being a settlement at the mouth of the River Ems which rapidly developed as a port to which the population of Warblington migrated. Trade with the continent in wool and wine brought prosperity, an annual fair and weekly market being granted in 1239. Once noted for oysters, Emsworth's trade received a fatal blow at the beginning of the nineteenth century when it was alleged that Emsworth oysters eaten at a Winchester banquet carried typhoid, after an infection resulted in fatalities. The town, now a busy yachting centre, has facilities for boat-building and other allied industries. Much of its former character may be seen on the water-front and in Tower Street and King Street. Langstone Harbour, a well-kept group of Georgian and early nineteenth-century houses and quay walls, served Havant as a port. Two public houses and a tide mill combined with a windmill tower create a picturesque and popular scene. To reach Hayling Island, one must cross over a narrow channel, Sweare Deep, by a bridge at this point.

Favoured as a holiday resort the island has a fine safe sandy

Warblington church

Langstone Harbour

beach extending along its southern shore. Following the construction of the bridge across the channel at Langstone in 1822-4 a crescent and a few villas were built prematurely in anticipation of the development of the island as a resort, which did not actually occur until the 1930s.

The picturesque church of North Hayling has a shingled belfry and spirelet unusually placed at the east end of the nave. Said to lack conventional foundations but built upon 'large boulders', presumably sarsen stones, this is the possible cause of the movement of the chancel east wall which was buttressed in the late seventeenth century. Inside, the framework of the bell-turret, which contains three bells dated 1350, has an associated arched beam across the east bay of the nave carved with cusps and pierced tracery.

South Hayling church of St Mary's, in the popular southern region of the island, was built by the Abbey of Jumièges in Normandy which held the manor of South Hayling. It dates from the thirteenth century and combines a tall nave with a low central tower crowned by a shingled broach spire. Several features are exceptionally fine—the windows of the aisles are little-restored, and those to the east are particularly notable. The chancel, Early English and the first section of the church to be built has a double piscina.

176

11 Portsmouth

Portsea Island, upon which the city of Portsmouth stands, is bounded by Portsmouth Harbour to the west and Langstone Harbour to the east; a creek to the north, beneath a new road construction, separates the island from the mainland. Portsmouth developed from a small settlement established on the eastern shore of the Camber, a sea-water lake, in the south-west corner of the island, which extended eastward to a line approximately from Portsmouth High Street to the Guildhall. The value of the position of this settlement as a place of embarkation for France was appreciated by the Norman kings, but development did not occur until the late twelfth century. Evidence is not lacking of the city's subsequent growth as a commercial port and, more importantly, as a naval dockyard.

From Havant the coast road passes the Great Salterns golf course before turning inland, leaving Eastney to the south-east. Development occurred at Eastney in the nineteenth century and in the 1860s the Royal Marine Barracks was built. It is a large complex of brick buildings; the officers' mess has a stone fronted façade with the main entrance on the first floor opening into an Italianate porch approached by a balustraded stairway. At the junction of Henderson Road and Bransbury Road, near the Royal Marine Barracks, is Eastney Pumping Station—built of brick and housing a Boulton and Watt reciprocal steam-engine installed in 1887. A building nearby houses Crossley Gas Engines. The Royal Marine Museum and the Pumping Station are open to the public.

Fort Cumberland, on a spit of land east of the Pumping Station and commanding the narrow channel into Langstone Harbour, was built with convict labour in 1746 by the Duke of Cumberland. Its design was changed by the Duke of Richmond in 1786 as he wished to make it part of a larger scheme, but Parliament rejected his ideas by the Speaker's casting vote. Gibbon wrote of the fort, 'To raise this bulwark at enormous price, The head of folly used the hand of vice.' The building is now of historical importance as one of the best eighteenth-century star-fortresses to have survived in Britain. At the time of writing it is not open to the public.

From Eastney, Southsea Esplanade extends along the seafront past pleasure gardens to South Parade Pier, designed by G.E. Smith and built in 1908-9. Badly damaged by fire, it has been restored to its former Edwardian elegance and has a gilt and red plush music-hall, a tea-room, and an open air bandstand. From the pier-end ships take holiday-makers on trips and fishermen cast their lines to un-cooperative fish.

Southsea Castle to the west of the pier was built in 1544 and is a square fort contained within enceinte walls forming a larger square set diamond-fashion in relation to it. At the east and west angles of the enceinte large rectangular gun platforms were an innovation at the time as the fort was one of the first to be built expressly for the use of guns.

The castle was part of the fortifications built by Henry VIII— following the anxiety caused by the reconciliation of Francis I with Charles V in 1538, and the prospect of their joint invasion to impose the Catholic will upon Henry. As it happened, Francis and Charles quarrelled again by 1540 and the threat to England diminished. During the Civil War the castle was taken by Parliamentary troops and the action ended Royalist support in Portsmouth. In 1759 extensive internal damage was caused by an explosion and repairs were carried out in 1800. Alterations were made in 1814-16 and from 1844-50 it was used as a prison. With fear of trouble from France again in 1850 it was once more used as a fortress.

Southsea Common is laid out with gardens, tennis courts and a skating rink. Rock gardens have been created to landscape the area around the castle, from which there are panoramic views across Spithead with Spitbank Fort and Horse Sand Fort out in the channel to be seen against the background of the Isle of Wight.

The anchor of HMS *Victory* stands by the esplanade and east-wards is Clarence Pier, a lively, noisy place with snack bars and stalls supplying fish and chips, shellfish, sweets and souvenirs. The large Amusement Park provides all the thrills of a modern fun-fair.

Beyond the Amusement Park are sections of the old Ports-mouth defences. These include the Kings Bastion and Long Curtain, the Saluting Platform, the Square Tower, the Eighteen

Portsmouth: an ornate beach shelter with the anchor of HMS Victory *in the background*

Gun Battery and the Round Tower—an exciting waterfront composition.

The Square Tower was built in 1494 as part of the fortifications of the Camber; it may also have been a residence for the military governor. The tower was reduced in height and used as a powder magazine from the late sixteenth century until the end of the eighteenth century when it became a meat store for the Navy. It was faced in stone in the 1820s and a semaphore station was established on top of it—the end of the line of semaphores from the Admiralty in Whitehall. The bust of Charles I set in a circular recess is by Le Sueur and was presented by Charles to mark his landing after travels in France and Spain.

The Round Tower stands at the narrowest point of the channel between Portsmouth and Gosport. It is entered from Broad Street, and stairs lead past gun emplacements to the tower, from the top of which can be seen Portsmouth Harbour, with Tower House and the houses of The Point in the foreground. The Submarine Museum, HMS *Dolphin,* and the Haslar Royal Naval Hospital at Gosport are across the channel where the shoreline runs out to Gilkicker Point.

The Point and Tower House, Portsmouth

Part of the Round Tower is probably early fifteenth century, other sections date from Henry VIII's time, the Napoleonic period, and the mid-nineteenth century, when the top was reconstructed. A similar tower was built at Gosport, and in 1522 a chain was extended between them as a boom to protect the harbour. The curtain wall westward from the Square Tower to the Round Tower was designed by de Gomme for Charles II. A Sally Port was provided to give access to the sea from Broad Street.

180

These works are only a fraction of the formidable fortifications which once encircled the city, but by 1870 they were obsolete and nearly all swept away. From near Clarence Pier, bastions, ravelins and dry moats extended northward; running east of Pier Road, Bellevue Terrace and Kings Terrace, they turned along Museum Road, George's Road—where the Landport Gate provided the main landward entrance—and finally to Gun Wharf Road and the Camber at the Town Quay.

The need for defences at Portsmouth began in the early fourteenth century when its value as a naval dockyard and

The Jubilee Tavern, Bellevue Terrace, Portsmouth

harbour convenient for the French coast made it equally vulnerable to French harassment. Attacks in 1339, 1369 and 1377 were destructive and vicious and a Royal Commission in 1386 recommended the building of substantial earth ramparts and wood structures.

In the mid-nineteenth century, following Louis Napoleon's successful *coup d'état* in 1851 together with the threat of a fleet of iron-clads in Cherbourg dockyard, there was reason to expect trouble from France. A Royal Commission therefore recommended strengthening of the defences, including reinforcement of cover for Spithead by building forts in Spithead itself. Land cover was provided by a line of forts to the west of Gosport together with forts along Portsdown Hill. Lord Palmerston was the Prime Minister of the time and he put these plans into effect between 1857 and 1880. Five forts, plus one at Fareham, defended Gosport from the west. Six stood on Portsdown Hill and four— after some difficulties—were built in Spithead. All the work was completed by 1880 but by then the tension was completely relaxed. The fortifications became known as Pam's Folly, and Portsmouth had the dubious honour of being the last city in Europe to receive a ring of fortifications which were medieval in conception—and obsolete on completion.

The construction of the fortifications before 1870 and the billeting of a garrison caused serious overcrowding within the old town, and development outside the walls began in the early eighteenth century. This reflected the increasing importance and growth of the dockyard, and housing developments of mostly terraced property spread to Portsea, Landport, Southsea, Fratton and Eastney. The housing varies from the poorest type to good artisan houses and to large terraces such as Bellevue, Landport and Hampshire in Southsea.

During the 1830s and 50s Thomas Ellis Owen, builder, speculator and architect, took part in the extension of Southsea's development with a series of stuccoed terraces. One of his earliest rows of houses—perhaps his best—is that containing numbers twenty-nine to forty Kent Road, and Portland Terrace of 1846 is his most pretentious.

Jane Austen knew Portsmouth—she had two brothers who were naval officers in Nelson's time—and in *Mansfield Park* she describes Sunday morning walks on the ramparts taken by the Price family after attending service at the Royal Garrison Church. This church was part of the *Domus Dei*, founded in 1212 by the canons of Southwick Priory as a hospital for the sick and aged. The architectural arrangement of the building may have been similar to other establishments, with the nave and aisles used as hospital living accommodation and the chancel set apart as a chapel. The building fell into disrepair after the Dissolution, but was restored to serve the garrison when a military governor's house was built next to it in the late sixteenth century. The governor's house was demolished in 1827 and in 1866 the church was restored by G.E. Street. The nave was badly damaged by fire in the 1940 air raids and stands now as a preserved ruin, but the chancel survived and is still in use.

The area to the south-west of Garrison Church, which remains an open space, was used for military parades and old photographs show scenes with Sunday morning strollers watching the assembled soldiers on church parade. Another parade-ground was Governor's Green where Trooping the Colour by the Hampshire Regiment is recorded by a photograph of the late nineteenth century.

After the devastation of the last war only a little of the character of old Portsmouth High Street has survived. There has been residential development which is pleasant, and in scale with surviving nineteenth century, and earlier, buildings. The George Inn, from which Nelson departed by a back door into Penny Street to avoid cheering crowds as he left Portsmouth for the last time, has been destroyed but the attractive early nineteenth-century Dolphin Hotel remains. It has a Greek Doric porch flanked at the first and second floors with shallow bay windows linked above by a bold dentil moulding beneath a projecting cornice. Buckingham House nearby has a late sixteenth-century framed structure with a stuccoed eighteenth-century front. Formerly the Spotted Dog, it is the house where George Villiers, Duke of Buckingham, was murdered by John Felton on 23 August 1628. As adviser to Charles I he was making preparations for a force to relieve La Rochelle, and unpaid, undisciplined soldiers were mutinous. Felton was executed at Tyburn and his body brought back to Portsmouth and hanged in chains on the beach. A memorial to Villiers by Nicholas Stone was erected in the cathedral by his sister.

Portsmouth Grammar School is at the northern end of High Street and occupies the former Cambridge Barracks built in 1855-60. The school moved there in 1926 from a site at the corner of Cambridge Road and St George's Road which it had occupied since 1878. Cambridge Barracks is a plain, unadorned building, forty bays long and with one upper storey. A Royal Arms in stone stands on the parapet above the main entrance. A dour but admirable building, it dominates this end of High Street which is enlivened by a pair of brick houses with parapets and dormers. There is also a pompous grey stucco Victorian house with a surfeit of Greek fret ornament—a house to be looked at twice, if only for its audacity.

Along St George's Road leading from nearby Cambridge Junction is the Landport Gate, the only town gate left in place when the fortifications were demolished. It dates to 1760 and is attributed to Hawksmoor. Another gate, St James Gate, which stood across Broad Street before The Point, is in nearby Burnaby Road.

Warblington Street leads to the Camber and a group of streets worth exploring. In Lombard Street numbers one, three and five have three shaped gables: they are mid-seventeenth century and of brick subsequently stuccoed. Window openings in the south and central gables appear to be little altered, but the other openings—including the doors—may be eighteenth- and nine-teenth-century alterations. The original window openings would have had mullions and transoms. The deep bay window below the end gable is unusual for Portsmouth, where much shallower bays such as those at numbers seven and nine in the same street were favoured. Number seven has a good doorcase and a segmental bay, number nine has a curved bay. More town houses are in St Thomas Street facing the west end of the cathedral: they are larger than those in Lombard Street but of similar date.

The Cathedral Church of St Thomas, made a cathedral in 1927, stands on a site in High Street surrounded by lawns. The building is of three periods, the earliest is 1196 and includes the choir and transepts built by the canons of Southwick Priory. The original west tower was destroyed, along with the nave and aisles, in a bombardment during the Civil War, and were rebuilt in the 1680s. The cupola was added in 1702 but the weathervane is a replica of the original dated 1710 which was blown down in 1954 and is in the cathedral. Work was carried out in the 1930s by Sir Charles Nicholson, who was given the task of enlarging the existing building with a western addition without removing the tower. It was difficult to bring existing work into any relation-ship with new—the central tower prevented it—unless some means could be found of opening its lower section whilst still supporting the upper. Sir Charles compromised, and spaces on either side of the tower—between the aisles of the new nave and those of the old choir— were created. The scheme has not worked. There is a church east of the tower, and a meeting

Nos. 7 and 9, Lombard Street, Portsmouth

room west of it. The work begun in the 1930s is not finished, and new plans, prepared in 1966, propose to add modern constructions and materials.

St Thomas Street leads to Oyster Street, White Hart Road,

The Cathedral Church of St Thomas, Portsmouth

186

Broad Street and The Point. East of Broad Street the Camber is industrialized, but to the west it is different, especially around Bath Square where small town houses have been repaired and painted to good effect. Appropriately, there are three public houses of the eighteenth or early nineteenth centuries here. A weatherboarded house—Quebec House, dated 1754—adds to the scene and stands over the water. It was built as a sea-water bath house when sea bathing was beginning to gain popularity for its medical value, but before bathing in public was socially acceptable. The distinctive Tower House, seen in my drawing, has become a landmark almost as well known as the Semaphore Tower in the dockyard. The house was the home of W.L. Wylie RA, the marine painter, examples of whose work are to be seen in Portsmouth Art Gallery.

When it is busy with holiday visitors The Point regains something of its old character. In the few acres around the Camber ships have been built and broken up, and the victorious have been cheered. The inhabitants of The Point were referred to as the Spice Islanders, either because of their personal odour, or that of the place. It was the resort of both high and low in all walks of life but especially the Navy. All were served and all wants provided. Eating houses, cookshops, cheapjacks, pawnbrokers, tailors, jewellers, watchmakers—they were all concentrated there in the smallest imaginable space, the more to create a remarkable assemblage of jostling and thieving humanity. Some were courageous, some were famous, many were vagabonds yet some were of noble birth—but mostly all had business in connection with the sea.

The Main Gate into HM Dockyard is at the end of The Hard, north of The Point. It has two Portland stone piers surmounted by gold spheres, and once had a wrought-iron gate. The width of the opening—wide enough to take a loaded wagon—had to be increased in 1943 and the iron gates were taken away. The red-brick wall which follows the perimeter of the dockyard north-eastwards from the gate was built in 1704-11 and is nearly three-quarters of mile long.

The Main Gate is the entrance for visitors to HMS *Victory* and the *Mary Rose*. The walk through the dockyard takes the visitor past several buildings of interest. Inside the gate is a lodge, now the Police Office; built in 1708, it is one of the oldest buildings within the docks. Boathouse number six, seen across the Old Mast Pond, was built in 1843 as a Mast House. It is in stock brick with three storeys and nine bays divided into three sections of three bays each—the centre three project slightly forward. It is

akin to St George's Church in St George's Square—completely utilitarian—and a superb design emerges depending upon proportion and the arrangement of vertical and horizontal divisions: the stone string course between the ground and first floor ties the composition together. The three large round-headed openings on the ground floor add a final touch of nobility to the design. The interior has been described as having a cast-iron structure supporting the floors, the whole designed to carry considerable weights.

The Point, Portsmouth

Next, numbers nine, ten and eleven stores are of 1787. These three blocks are typical of the fine buildings of this period in the dockyard—plain and unadorned but deriving great dignity thereby. Number ten, the centre block, had a clocktower which formed a climax to the vista from Anchor Lane opposite. This was lost by bombing, but the rusticated stone central archway provides a central focus for the group. To the south-west it is possible to glimpse the Semaphore Tower built in 1926-9, so-called because it is crowned by a replica in stone of

189

St George's Church, Portsmouth

the nineteenth-century Semaphore Tower. It is a landmark associated with the dockyard and views of Portsmouth from the harbour and Spithead.

In Stoney Lane, opposite the 1787 stores, is the rope house. It is just short of a third of a mile long, a great stretch of Georgian brick punctuated only by the progression of windows on three storeys. This was the building set on fire by Jack the Painter in 1776, but it was reconstructed in 1960 when the end elevations were rebuilt and the dormers removed. The loss of the latter has spoilt the effect and left the building monotonous.

Finally, St Anne's Church, east of the rope house, is occasionally open to the public. It was built in 1785-6, but the west end was badly damaged by bombing and restored in 1955. The nave was shortened in the restoration and the west end and cupola were rebuilt to the original design. It is plain outside, but charming and elegant within.

The purpose of entering the dockyard along the route I have described is to visit the cafeteria, the museums, HMS *Victory* and the *Mary Rose*. Visitors must keep to the prescribed footpaths, and only the *Victory* may be photographed.

HMS *Victory*, flagship of the Commander-in-Chief, Naval Home Command, was built at Chatham in 1759 and launched in May 1765. She remained in the Medway until 1778, when she became the flagship of Admiral Keppel. She subsequently wore the flags of successive admirals and fought against revolutionary France.

In 1797 HMS *Victory* returned to Chatham and was a hospital ship in the Medway until 1801 when she underwent a refit and was redesigned. By 1803 she was Nelson's flagship in the Mediterranean, assisting to form the course of events which culminated in 1805 at Trafalgar, where Nelson was in the thick of the battle. She was badly damaged, but was put under tow to Gibraltar for emergency repairs and subsequently brought Nelson's body to Sheerness, from whence it was conveyed to Greenwich to lie in state in the Painted Hall before interment in St Paul's Cathedral. After a refit at Chatham and some service, HMS *Victory* was berthed at Portsmouth until 1922, by which time her deterioration caused anxiety. An appeal was launched and she was put in Number Two Dock—the site of the oldest graving dock in the world. As I write restoration to the appearance she had at Trafalgar is in progress, and work will be completed by 1987.

The sight of this magnificent ship at close quarters is unforgettable. It is a reminder of the selfless devotion to country of naval men before, and since, Nelson's time. The size of the ship is staggering, especially when one remembers that it is constructed of wood. That it was but one of a great number of similar—if less famous—ships, makes the achievements of the shipwrights awe-inspiring. Theirs was a skill, which on this scale, has died out. Their finest ships have virtually all gone, but survivors such as HMS *Victory* remind us that carpenters engaged in architectural timber construction did not, by any means, produce the only large-scale masterpieces in wood.

HMS Victory, *Portsmouth*

English domination of the Channel and the occupation of Boulogne spurred the French to retaliate in 1545, and they sent a fleet of ships, including troop transports, with the intention of breaking English domination of the Channel and obtaining a foothold on the Isle of Wight.

The English and French navies were tactically different: the French had galleys with a battering-ram and forward-facing cannon; the English ships were designed to fire broadside. Neither adversary was very efficient and much manoeuvring took place without either gaining an advantage. The *Mary Rose* was lost, not by enemy action but, it is thought, because of bad design. This ship had been converted from a merchantman and gun-ports had been placed too near the water-line. These were open, with guns drawn out when the ship keeled over—perhaps in a sudden gust of wind; the sea poured in and she foundered very quickly with much loss of life. During recent years the wreck has been excavated and many items of historical interest found. A section of the hull was subsequently raised and this, together with other finds, is displayed in the museum near HMS *Victory*.

The Beneficial School in Kent Street between The Hard and Ordnance Row was built in 1784 as a free school for boys and for social gatherings. The first floor was the schoolroom, and is lit by a Venetian window flanked on each side by a window. St George's Square nearby contains one or two houses of the early eighteenth-century and later, but St George's Church claims most attention. Badly damaged during the war but beautifully restored, it dates from 1754 and is almost contemporary with the building of HMS *Victory* at Chatham. Its unsophisticated, workmanlike appearance must be credited to the fifteen dock-yard shipwrights who built it, for although the plan is complex it lacks all fussiness and depends for success upon the management of plain brick surfaces and roof lines. The fenestration, an integral part of the design, is used with telling directness and simplicity and the composition is surmounted at the west end by a bell-turret, again robust and simple.

The area near the church contains much new housing, mostly in the form of moderate-sized terraced dwellings grouped with plenty of space around them. The result is a very pleasant 'human' scale—such a house could be a 'home'. Also, near the Beneficial School, a warehouse and a late Georgian house with a very attractive doorcase are interesting survivals which I hope will be retained.

When the growing town of Portsea was brought within the

393 Commercial Road, Portsmouth: the birthplace of Charles Dickens

fortifications, Unicorn Gate was built in 1778 as a town gate. In 1865 it was taken down and somewhat altered when rebuilt as a gate to the rapidly-expanding dockyard. It can only be seen from outside the dockyard in Unicorn Road. This is north of the Guildhall, built in 1886-90 by William Hill, which forms a focal point in Commercial Road, the main shopping centre of Portsmouth.

After the fortifications of the old town had been swept away in the 1870s the communities of Portsea and Portsmouth began to merge and as development gained momentum across the island the logical choice of a site for a Guildhall was to the north of the ancient settlement. The building was wrecked by bombing and has been restored. The impressive steps to the entrance portico remains, also the frontage, raised upon a rusticated ground storey with attached colonnades rising two storeys to an entablature and balustrade. The composition is topped by a central tower of three stages, with a belfry stage and clock above. The original cupola which completed the design was not replaced, and neither were the flanking turrets at the corners which were similar to those remaining near the tower.

North of Charlotte Street shopping centre along Commercial Road stands All Saints Church built by Jacob Owen in 1827-8. A remarkable use of cast iron may be seen in the nave: iron piers support plaster vaulting and the interior is exciting and original, comparable to the best examples of Victorian Gothic I have seen anywhere. The decoration has been well chosen to enhance its charm.

A short distance north of All Saints at 393, Commercial Road, the birthplace of Charles Dickens is now a museum, displaying Dickensian memorabilia. Born at the house in 1812 the author lived there for only two years, as his parents moved to another house in the town before finally leaving to live in London. A public house nearby is named—inevitably—Oliver Twist.

12   From Portchester to Netley Abbey

Portsdown, the narrow ridge of chalk north of Portsmouth, forms a backcloth north of a coastal strip traversed by the busy M27 and A27. From its spine may be seen a wide panorama, including Portsmouth Harbour, with Portchester Castle easily identifiable on a promontory forming a contrast with modern towers and structures to which from here distance can lend enchantment.

Portchester Castle has a superb site ten feet above sea level and bordered on two sides by the sea on a spit of land at the head of Portsmouth Harbour. Continuous fortification walls some eighteen feet high and ten feet thick, built by the Romans in the late third century, enclose a 'square' of about nine acres. Sections of walling are so little changed that the method of Roman construction of coursed flint rubble bonded with courses of tile or stone may be studied. Of the original twenty bastions equally spaced along the perimeter and at the angles, fourteen remain. Principal gates stand centrally in the east and west walls, posterns to the north and south.

The purpose of the castle was to defend the coast from raiding Saxons—part of a defensive system extending from the Wash to Southampton Water placed under the command of the 'Count of the Saxon Shore'. Military concentration increased when a commander of the Channel Fleet, Carausius, usurped the rule of Rome making himself Emperor in 286. He was supplanted by Allectus in 296, who in turn was defeated by Constantius Chlorus in the same year. Military occupation finally ceased about 369 when forces were transferred to Bitterne.

Recent excavation has proved that the fort also served as a large supply base, with barns and granaries and an important import and export centre for Roman Britain. There is evidence of Saxon occupation, and in the late twelfth century the Normans built a keep in the north-west corner, which had a fortified inner bailey containing domestic buildings. During the fourteenth century these buildings were replaced, or greatly improved, by Richard II who unfortunately did not live to enjoy them.

The dramatic Roman towers of Portchester Castle

197

By the seventeenth century the keep was ruinous, although part of the domestic range was complete. Subsequently the castle was sold to private ownership, but leased back from time to time for the accommodation of prisoners of war—including those of the Napoleonic Wars.

In 1133 Henry I founded a priory of Austin Canons in the south-east corner of the Roman walls, but for reasons that can only be guessed at, probably lack of space, they left within a very short time and moved to Southwick. The priory church, now also the parish church, remains within the castle walls but the monastic buildings have gone. With the known dates of the foundation, 1133, and the departure for Southwick, 1145-53, it can be assumed that the church was completed by around 1150; thus it is a very useful dated building for comparative study.

A canon regular of St Augustine

The work is of high quality, and since it is late Norman it does not show the brashness of the early conquerors. The west front is restrained, indeed elegant—an adjective seldom appropriate for Norman work. Especially beautiful is the stiff leaf ornament of the capitals below the arches at the crossing.

Southwick, the place to which the Portchester canons repaired, is below the northern side of Portsdown Hill, a pleasantly remote place of thatched cottages where modern development has been almost entirely held at bay—at least up to now. Southwick Priory held considerable lands and exerted much influence in the area—Henry VI married Margaret of Anjou there in 1445, and in Portsmouth the abbey founded the *Domus Dei* and the church of St Thomas, later the cathedral.

At the Dissolution the priory buildings were given to John Whyte, who has been described as a mean, fawning servant of Wriothesley, Earl of Southampton. He pulled down part of the priory and turned the remaining monastic buildings into his house. Following his death the estate passed to his son, and then to Sir Daniel Norton. Sir Daniel's son, who succeeded his father, sided with Parliament, but obviously not too energetically, for he earned from Cromwell the nickname 'Idle Dick'.

John Whyte's house was burnt down in 1750 and replaced by another, this also destroyed by fire in 1812. The present house replaced it in 1841. It is now HMS *Dryad*—the headquarters of General Eisenhower when he gave the order to commence the D-Day landings on 6 June 1944.

Southwick Priory church has gone but the parish church was restored—or almost rebuilt—by John Whyte in 1566. It is therefore a rare example of early post-Reformation church building. The interior fittings are mostly pre-eighteenth century. The pews in the nave had to be replaced in 1955, but the three-decker pulpit and large box pews in the chancel used by the squire and his household remain, as do the west gallery and the reredos. A monument to John Whyte and his wife in the north chapel has late Gothic decoration—not to be confused with Gothic Revival work.

The parish church of Southwick, rebuilt in 1566

Southwick church, referred to as the 'Peculiar of Southwick', is not subject to diocesan or other jurisdiction, but nevertheless, it adheres to the doctrine of the Church of England.

The church of St Nicholas at Boarhunt has been combined with Southwick since 1369 and is a highly important late Saxon building. There is no village, and the church stands near Manor Farm on the northern slopes of Portsdown Hill above Southwick. It dates from *c.* 1064, although a broader estimate of 950-1100 by Taylor and Taylor, which allows some latitude, is more acceptable.

The building lacks the tall, narrow proportions of early Saxon work untouched by Norman influences but its structure has survived with only minor alteration. Covered in places with plaster, the nave is of flint, with Binstead stone quoins. The chancel is also of flint. There is no long and short work, and no lesenes, but an unusual horizontal string course across the east gable with a vertical strip above extending to the apex. This feature is believed to exist, obscured by later stonework, on a Saxon church at Kirkdale in Yorkshire and confidently dated to between 1055 and 1065 by an inscription—hence the date of *c.* 1064 suggested for St Nicholas.

There is a superb double splayed Saxon window in the north wall of the chancel. It is blocked inside by a monument, but the external splay is visible, and there is also a stone mid-wall slab cut out as a frame for the window opening, decorated with wheat-ear moulding. Inside the church the chancel arch is semicircular, and although not constructed with through stones, it has stripwork carried round the head which continues as pilaster-strips down to the floor—a feature typical of Saxon work. There are capitals, formed of four horizontal bands of moulding for the imposts of the arch and the stripwork. Saxon entrance doors in the south and north nave walls can be traced, and evidence has been found of a former wall across the nave which created a small western chamber.

Above Boarhunt lanes traverse the spine of the chalk escarpment, where from Nelson's monument there are breathtaking views over Portsmouth Harbour. Fareham can be entered near Fort Wallington, one of the Portsdown forts which after many vicissitudes is now a store and not open to the public. Once favoured by retired naval officers, Fareham flourished in the eighteenth century as a market town and small port. There is little doubt that High Street ranks as one of the finest country-town streets in Hampshire—some would say in the whole of the south of England. At its southern end, near to its junction with

West Street, it was wide enough to form a market-place in medieval times, but with the passing of time encroachment formed an island site which created a back street—now Union Street.

High Street has many houses built during the prosperous eighteenth century. Some are of deep red brick—'Fareham reds'—for which the town has been famous since the seventeenth century. There is also a façade of mathematical tiles. The County Club has large curved bays typical of the late eighteenth century, and a handsome porch with a pedimented hood supported by Tuscan columns. At the north end of High Street the Old Manor House is early eighteenth century with a simple but exquisite brick façade, and a porch with a curved hood, pedimented and supported on Corinthian columns.

The parish church—St Peter and St Paul—has stood on its present site near the High Street since Saxon times and has changed very much over the centuries. Part of the Saxon church remains in the lower walls of the eastern section of the Early English north chapel. Long and short work at the northeast corner survives, as do the north and east walls of a former Saxon chancel. The present chancel is by Blomfield, about 1888, and was to be part of his scheme to rebuild a nave of 1812. This he did not do, it was left to Sir Charles Nicholson, who, it is generally agreed, produced a nave which gives a feeling of space and light. The tower, capped with a cupola built in 1742, displays the local blue brick effectively with Fareham 'reds' used as dressings.

Bishopswood, west of the town, was enlarged about 1900 in the cottage orné style; it is reminiscent of Blaize Hamlet. A large thatched house with wide eaves supported upon rustic posts, a well planned and proportioned Gothic fenestration of wood with slender tracery increases its charm and eccentricity.

In the seventeenth century Fareham Harbour, a creek of Portsmouth Harbour, was described as 'an absolute good and safe place to moor ships', and the port did considerable trade in coal, timber, Fareham bricks and pottery until the nineteenth century. With the increasing interest in small leisure ships, the harbour has yards catering for the new sport.

Gosport was contained within strong defensive walls, complementary to those of Portsmouth across the entrance of Portsmouth Harbour, and indeed the defences were physically linked at one time by an iron chain that extended between towers on the opposite shores. During the bombing of the last war much of Gosport, crowded within the old defences, was

Fareham High Street

destroyed, and this gave an opportunity to re-develop the area. However, many buildings of interest remain. The Royal Clarence Victualling Yard in Weevil Lane—so called for obvious reasons— has a grand entrance gateway of 1828. The campanile of Holy Trinity, a Gosport landmark, was designed by Sir Arthur

202

Blomfield in 1889 who completely restored the church, trans-
forming the exterior into a north Italian basilica.

Built in 1696 as a chapel of ease for the parish church of
Alverstoke, Holy Trinity was enlarged in 1734 and 1835.
However, the nave of 1696 remains, in Classical style with

Centre bay of The Crescent at Alverstoke, built in 1826

colonnades of Ionic columns supporting a deep entablature. The columns were turned from single oak trunks. The church stands surrounded by tall modern blocks and one has to admire the derivative work of Blomfield in preference to the boring constructions that surround it.

Alverstoke, now part of a continuous development with Gosport, was originally a small village on the Haslar Creek until the early nineteenth century, when the Marquess of Anglesey sponsored a scheme to turn Alverstoke into a seaside town. The extent of the plans is not known, but a few buildings were erected, including The Crescent of 1826, which has a grand, nineteen bay, gently curving façade. Other buildings which were part of this scheme also survive, including a small house in a street at the rear of The Crescent, which I am told was used by the contractor during the course of building The Crescent and other villas in the area.

Lee-on-the-Solent grew as a seaside resort in the late nineteenth century—it had a railway station and a pier—now both gone. Its architectural interest depended upon Lee Tower, a 1935 building in concrete which was demolished in 1969. Erosion of the shore by the sea has been a blessing to Lee, as a sea-wall was built which forms a long promenade beloved of holidaymakers and anglers alike.

The coast north-west of Lee is not memorable, except for the interest derived from shipping in the Solent. Hill Head, Stubbington, Crofton and Titchfield Haven have all suffered from urban development. It is said that the roof of Crofton church may 'possibly' contain ships' timbers.

Hamble, a fishing-village long before the leisure-mariners came, gained a living from oysters, lobsters and crabs taken from the Solent. The priory, a cell of the Abbey of Thiron, near Chartres, fared well on fishing—the monks supplied St Swithun's at Winchester with twenty thousand oysters for Lent in exchange for goods. The priory church is now Hamble parish church.

In the nineteenth century Hamble, and later Warsash, provided facilities for the distribution of shellfish to London from the west country, Ireland and France. Large tanks in which to keep the fish were built at Warsash, and specially constructed boats, with sieve-like tanks open to the sea, were used to transport them.

Ships and shipbuilding have played an important part in the history of Hamble River. It was important for the building of Navy ships from the seventeenth century until the coming of iron. Philemon Ewer had a yard at Bursledon where he built the *Falkland* and the *Ruby* in the late eighteenth century. George Parsons had a yard near the Jolly Sailor where he built the *Elephant*, the ship in which Nelson served at the Battle of Copenhagen when he put the glass to his blind eye.

The Bugle, Hamble

The abbey at Netley on the western shore of the Hamble River was loved by poets and writers who became lyrical upon visiting the place when the crumbling abbey was overgrown with ivy. Walpole referred to it as paradise, while D.H. Moutray Read in his *Highways and Byways in Hampshire* comments 'very beautiful, but with the sadness that pertains to all ruins'. The present fashion among young archaeologists is not for picturesque ruins, and the Ministry of Public Works have rightly cut down the ivy and the undergrowth and work continues on the walls to arrest further decay. However, I wonder if neat gardening—as opposed to necessary maintenance—can be overdone.

Netley, like Salisbury which is almost contemporary with it, was built in one mighty burst of energy when the Early English period attained greatness. Monks from Beaulieu moved to Netley in 1239 and in 1251 Henry III became their patron—an inscription on a foundation stone at the base of the north-east pier of the crossing records his name. Work began about 1240—when Salisbury was still in the building—and the nave was almost complete by 1300.

The confidence and speed with which such works of excellence were completed is staggering. The size of the church is considerable and the design restrained. The three arches of the

206

chapter house typify the style of the building and rely upon proportion and simple mouldings for their effect.

Following the Dissolution, Netley was acquired by Sir William Paulet who made a house within the church. Brickwork in the ruins is all that remains of this house, probably taken down with parts of the abbey in the early eighteenth-century after it had been sold by Sir Berkeley Lucy to a Southampton carpenter called Taylor. Taylor had a dream foretelling his death on the site: this did not deter him from demolition, but falling tracery from the great west window landed on his head and proved to be the final deterrent!

The standing walls of the church are those of the chancel and the south transept, also the aisle walls of the nave. The nave arcades and clerestory have gone. The north transept is also missing, but part of it survives in a garden folly at Cranbury Park—to the west of the A33 near Otterbourne—where it was re-erected with additions in about 1760.

William Cobbett described Botley near the head of Hamble River in the practical terms of a farmer. He wrote, 'lies in a valley, the soil of which is a deep stiff clay. Oak trees grow well; and this year the wheat grows well . . .' Nowadays chrysanthemums and strawberries grow there: not only well it seems, for they are available most months of the year.

In the High Street, where the porches of the Dolphin Hotel and the Bugle Hotel project over the pavement, there are some handsome Georgian houses. Botley House is a large eighteenth-century house in local red brick and the Market Hall was built in 1848, eight years after Cobbett's death, by the Farmers' Club, which he and his friend James Warner founded. I like to think that Cobbett would have approved of the hall, with its plain, no-nonsense Doric portico with a substantial entablature and pediment, the whole being crowned by a clock turret which lacks sophistication.

Bishop's Waltham, three miles north of Botley, has narrow streets and notable Georgian houses. Funners Bank, a plain late eighteenth-century house in High Street was latterly the only private bank in the country before its sale to Barclays in the early 1950s. Founded at the beginning of the nineteenth century, it served the market town and surrounding farmers. The church has been much restored, but the tower is early seventeenth-century Gothic, large and squat with Tudor-style windows.

Blanchard's Brickworks brought fame to the town when they produced bricks for Blackfriars Bridge and the Suez Canal. They specialized in terracotta, and possibly Coade Stone

The east end and south transept of Netley Abbey

Botley Market Hall

following a connection of M.H. Blanchard, then of Blackfriars Bridge Road, London, with the original Lambeth factory of Mrs Coade. They produced household pieces such as jugs and also staircases, in terracotta. One is tempted to speculate on the origin of various examples of artificial stone such as that at Deane and Harbridge, or the terracotta at Farringdon.

Mrs Eleanor Coade died in 1821 but the business continued. In 1855 M.H. Blanchard of Blackfriars Road advertised himself as being the successor to the Coade factory, but he does not seem to have survived for long. Were any of the 'secrets' of Coade passed to the Bishop's Waltham works?

The ruins of the Bishop's Palace, Bishop's Waltham

212

13   The Meon Valley

The River Meon enters the Solent at Titchfield Haven, where the Hampshire County Council has made a statutory Local Nature Reserve to protect the large numbers of wildfowl that frequent the area.

The river was navigable to the small port of Titchfield until 1611 when the third Earl of Southampton built a sea wall across the estuary to reclaim a large area of sea marsh. A pleasant, small town with evidence of past prosperity, there are many eighteenth-century buildings of brick in the High Street, notably the Bugle Hotel and the Queen's Head. The town also had a handsome timber-framed market hall built between 1600 and 1650 with an upper council chamber. It was moved to the rear of the Queen's Head where it sadly deteriorated to the point of becoming an alleged danger and a 'Dangerous Structure' notice was served by the local authority. The building was saved, but not for Titchfield, which was a pity, being re-erected at the Weald and Downland Open Air Museum in Sussex, which must be accorded the credit for its preservation. Many timber-framed houses survive in the town, however—there are two jettied houses in South Street with several others hidden by later refronting.

Church Street is a cul-de-sac ending at St Peter's Church, a building of exceptional interest at the lower part of the tower and west end of the nave are Saxon work of the eighth century. Writers have suggested the church may have been founded by Wilfred during his mission to the Meon valley in the seventh century, when he is thought to have founded churches at Corhampton and Warnford.

The Saxon church consisted of a west porch, a nave and a chancel. The west porch survives as the lower section of the present tower—it may originally have been of two storeys, but this is unknown. Built of rubble with quoins of Binstead stone—

Titchfield church

a limestone containing iron and tending to be rich dark brown in colour—the quoins are not set in a regular fashion. There is a bonding course of Roman bricks three deep round the tower and across the west end of the nave passing through the walls which are two feet three inches thick.

Similarity with Roman work in the Watergate at Portchester Castle can be seen in the west round-headed arch of the porch with through stone voussoirs of Binstead stone. The technique in managing the voussoirs at the springing of the arch, by angling them with a wedge of mortar, is comparable to work at Brixworth, Northamptonshire, date *c*. 700.

Within the porch, the east doorway is twelfth century Norman, with three orders of zigzag moulding and shafted jambs. The raising of the Saxon walls to form a tower is believed to date to this time also. A spire was added in the fifteenth century, and the wrought-iron gates were made at Funtley Ironworks two miles away.

Quoins at the south-west corner assist in determining the width of the Saxon nave—the north-west quoins are hidden, but the line of the high Saxon gable may be seen south of the tower. The length eastwards corresponds with the present nave—fifty-three feet—confirmed by remains of the Saxon chancel arch found in the lower section of the present arch.

214

A south aisle was added in the twelfth century and rebuilt in 1867. The chancel—rebuilt in the thirteenth-century and re-modelled in the fifteenth—is almost contemporary with the north aisle and arcade, a splendid example of Perpendicular architecture matched in quality by the monument in the south chapel. Of great importance as one of the most magnificent

Titchfield church tower

alabaster and marble monuments in Britain, the Wriothesley monument was erected early in the seventeenth century. One thousand pounds had been left by the second Earl of Southampton 'for two faire monuments' but only one was ever made, the contract for which is dated 1594.

An architectural composition of marble contains alabaster effigies of the first Earl and Countess of Southampton, as well as the second Earl with small figures representing his children, one of whom became the third Earl and a patron of Shakespeare. The work was executed by Gerard Johnson, a Flemish refugee, one of a group of sculptors working in London during the late sixteenth and seventeenth centuries. Gerard's son Nicholas, also a sculptor, probably assisted his father in the work.

Titchfield Abbey and the domestic range were converted into a house by Thomas Wriothesley, the first Earl of Southampton, who acquired the property following its dissolution. He was Henry VIII's Lord Chancellor at the time and well placed to get good pickings in the greedy scramble as abbeys and monasteries surrendered to the Crown. The White Canons of Titchfield following the Augustinian Rule were well versed in the knowledge of books and many valuable works were in their library. These vanished—did Wriothesley perhaps get more than the buildings?

Titchfield Abbey was founded in 1232 by Peter des Roches, Bishop of Winchester, as a house of Premonstratensian, or White, canons. These were so named after Prémontré in France, a group of White Canons from Halesowen in the Midlands being invited to settle there.

A White Canon

Place House, Titchfield

The abbey church had a central tower over an aisleless nave, but with aisled transepts. With the cloister unusually sited on the north side, Wriothesley constructed a gatehouse through the centre of the nave to give access, and made it the central courtyard of his house. The frater to the north of the cloister became his hall and the chapter house his chapel. The south transept and central tower of the abbey church were dismantled. Vaulting in the church was destroyed and floors inserted to provide upper rooms—fireplaces may be seen in upper walls of the nave and chancel. The transformation was completed by 1542—in only five years.

Following this conversion, when it became known as Place House, many notable people were entertained there including Edward VI, Mary I, Elizabeth I, and perhaps also Shakespeare. Conjecture goes further to suggest that *Romeo and Juliet* and other plays were given first performances there. Later Charles I arrived at the house, in his flight during November 1647, and well-meaning friends brought Colonel Robert Hammond to him. It was a fatal meeting for Charles . . . Place House continued to be occupied, and remained little altered, until the late eighteenth century when it fell into ruin and was used as a 'quarry', much of the material taken to build Cams Hall near Fareham. Overgrown and greatly deteriorated the ruins were placed in the care of the Ministry of Public Buildings and Works; they are tidy and preserved, but not so picturesque.

An iron industry flourished, at Funtley on the Meon, one and a half miles above Titchfield, and excavations in 1964 (by Mr Stephen Weeks) revealed the eighteenth-century works of Henry Cort, as well as evidence of the abbey's works. The Mill Master's House is timber-framed with an eighteenth-century brick addition. Great Funtley Farm—once the home of Samuel Jellicoe, Cort's partner—is a framed house with a continuous jetty and is possibly early sixteenth century. One of the earliest tilt-hammers was erected here in 1775 and part of the works output was bolts for the Navy, but they also made the iron gates under the tower of Titchfield church. Raw material for an iron-works was plentiful, ironstone is abundant in Christchurch cliffs and was 'harvested' on the coast where it rolled in on the surf—it was particularly plentiful on the coast near Beaulieu.

Founder of New College, Oxford—with Winchester College to complement it—William of Wykeham, one of the great edu-cationalists, Chancellor of England and Bishop of Winchester, was born at Wickham in 1324. There is probably nothing in the town of Wykeham's time, but The Square, with a small island site at the north-eastern end, is surrounded with many Georgian houses and a few early sixteenth-century buildings. They confirm that buildings of different periods and styles can enhance each other—but perhaps this theory works only if the modern planner and the twentieth century does not intervene. Knockers Bar at the north-west corner of The Square dates to the first half of the sixteenth century; it had a continuous jetty and there is evidence of a single bay open hall. A first-floor 'gallery' or passage crossed the hall, short joists serving both the jetty and the 'gallery'. Alexandra House, on the south-east side of The Square, has an eighteenth-century brick façade which conceals a small Wealden house extending into the adjoining property. The hall and one of the floored end bays has been identified.

Out of The Square and along Bridge Street, leading to the river and the railway, is Chesapeake Mill—so named by its builder John Prior in 1820 because it contains timber from the American warship of that name. Captured by the much smaller *Shannon* outside Boston Harbour in 1813, it was auctioned in Portsmouth Harbour and broken up.

At Shedfield, north-west of Wickham, a church of the 1870s faced with stone outside has an interior of multicoloured brick, some moulded. Also of brick, nearby is New Place a Lutyens house built in 1906 designed to preserve and contain the interiors of John Langton's seventeenth-century house which was to be

Chesapeake Mill, Wickham

demolished at Welsh Back, Bristol. The brick exteriors are plain, as I understand are the interiors. It seems that Lutyens set out to make a casket worthy of its contents.

Soberton is near the River Meon and its large sixteenth-century church tower rises above the valley. To the south along the A32 is St Clair's Farm in which a medieval upper floor hall of flint and stone has been incorporated into a house, first by the addition of a timber-framed wing to the north which was later followed by conversion into a double pile house by taking in the medieval work. There are mathematical tiles on east elevations. Nearby is a brick and chalk dovecote.

The parsonage near Droxford church was the home of Dr Hawkins, Izaak Walton's son-in-law, and in the house—now somewhat altered since his day—the old angler spent much of his later years. The village, very picturesque with many thatched cottages, stands to the north-west of the church on gently

219

rising ground. Georgian brick is evident—especially the local grey variety. Beacon House to the south was built in 1928—it has a thatched roof and a garden designed by Gertrude Jekyll.

The railway from Fareham to Alton was cut back to Droxford before its final demise in 1955, but the original plans envisaged a double track through Droxford to link Gosport and Portsmouth with Alton, Farnham and London. Time and the insidious internal combustion engine defeated the plans, but Droxford Station played an important role during the last war when it was necessary for the war leaders to meet and plan the D-Day invasion of Europe in June 1944. The headquarters was at Southwick. The idea was to work on a harmless-looking train up and down the railway line as it provided an unsuspicious moving target. Some time was spent in various tunnels.

Meonstoke is mercifully passed by the Alton to Fareham (A32) turnpike and left in contented isolation on the east bank of the Meon. From the church beside the river and the Bucks Head, the venue of the Manorial Courts long since extinguished, the street rises to the Coronation Tree at the crossing of the lanes and then descends, gently curving, to the school corner at the lower part of the village. The houses, built over four centuries, show themselves to advantage and each interacts with and enhances its neighbour, creating a pleasing composition. The additional interest of a thatched barn, aisled with a wagon porch, is a rare survival in a village street and is a reminder of the complete dependence of rural communities on the land in the past.

Corhampton church nearby, an extremely important late Saxon building, stands on a mound above the A32—a fine site which is perhaps even pre-Christian and which has survived with surprisingly little alteration. The east end was rebuilt in brick in 1855, after its collapse, which may have resulted from the removal of part of the mound for road-widening in the nineteenth century. The west gable has been repaired, also in brick, but most of the walls of the nave and the chancel are late Saxon work of about 1050-1100. They are of flint, thinly plastered, as was the Saxon custom. The openings, the lesenes, the long-and-short quoins at the corners of the nave and a plinth running round the original building, are all in dressed stone. It has been proposed by H.M. Taylor and Joan Taylor that the nave was higher, and that the original eaves were at a height corresponding with the string-course across the west gable. This would give another three feet or so to the height of the nave walls and provide room for horizontal string-courses forming an arcade by joining the tops of the existing lesenes.

There is a Saxon sundial on the south nave wall: it is circular with a vertical and a horizontal axis marked by rounded forms in relief. The diagonal lines are marked with a trefoil motif. These directions are incised across the horizontal diameter and there is a central hole for a gnomon.

Inside, the nave has a medieval crown-post roof and the Saxon chancel-arch is formed with through-stones. Voussoirs are laid with radial joints.

Exton is half a mile to the north of Corhampton and the church is worth visiting to see the font, Victorian Early English style in artificial stone which is possibly Coade stone.

Warnford Manor was held by Hugh de Port after the Conquest and an inscription records that Wilfred founded the church and Adam de Port restored it—this was in the twelfth century

The Saxon church at Corhampton

and corresponds with the style of the Norman tower. There is an indication of a previous narrower Saxon nave in the east wall of the tower, but apart from this only a Saxon sundial survives which is similar to the one at Corhampton.

West of the church is a King John's House. It had nothing to do with King John, but built in the thirteenth century it was a large aisled hall and the manor house of the de Port family, ancestors of the St Johns and Paulets. Although now very ruinous it was roofed until the eighteenth century when it was made into a picturesque ruin for the park of a newer house, Warnford Park, which was demolished soon after the Second World War leaving little or no trace. Above the road, almost opposite the entrance giving public access across the park to the church, is a fine Georgian brick house—the former parsonage.

A digression may be taken westwards from Warnford to the site of the deserted village of Lomar—an Ordnance Survey map will help the enthusiast find the place. Riversdown, a little to the north, has a large—indeed massive—base cruck surviving in a former open hall. A spere-truss also remains at what was the service end of the hall. The house is in private grounds and has little interest externally; permission to view the interior cannot be given except by special arrangement.

West Meon suffers from heavy traffic as many of the cottages and small houses abut the road. Garden Cottage, away from the main road, is a fine example of the older small houses in the village. Thatched and timber-framed, probably of the early or mid-seventeenth century, it was built as a hall house of three bays, the central bay open. Evidence points to an internal jetty that oversailed the hall at the west end. A chimney was later inserted in the eastern bay and the hall floored. Extensions to each end followed.

Warnford church

A lane leads north-west at an angle to the A32 and a triangular green is formed on which stands a war memorial. Cottages—some thatched—line the lane which rises gradually towards the church built by G.E. Street in 1843-6, in the churchyard of which can be found the grave of Thomas Lord. This was the Thomas Lord who owned the ground at St John's Wood later to become the headquarters of cricket. He retired here in 1830 to be a farmer—not because he had anything to do with Hampshire cricket. He died very shortly after his retirement.

The new-born River Meon emerges from the chalk at Oxenbourne below Hyden Hill, from whence it flows northward through East Meon beside the village street.

Some of the finest chalk country in the county provides a superb setting for East Meon church, which is exceptional for the quality of its architecture. The site is impressive—elevated above the village in a narrow churchyard scooped out of the side of Park Hill, part of the bishop's deer park which rises steeply behind it. So narrow is the site that there are no nave or chancel aisles to the north—although there is a north transept.

The manor of East Meon was a royal demesne from the time of its seizure by the Conqueror until it was granted to the Bishop of Winchester in the mid-twelfth century. However, Bishop Walkelin held the church in 1086 and he may have commenced the present building to replace a Saxon one. Bishop Henry de Blois saw the completion of the tower, which has three belfry windows on each face, all richly decorated with zigzag ornament; the broach spire is of a later date. The west door is also Norman and has a pair of shafts on each side, with simple leaf and fluted capitals and restrained zigzag ornament around the arch. It is a lovely thing, beautiful in design with colours and textures in the stonework that recall the water-colours of John Sell Cotman.

The interior focuses on the east and west arches of the crossing which have little ornament, being unusually plain for Norman work. There is much to see in this glorious church, but attention must be drawn to the Tournai marble font dating to the time of Henry de Blois and one of the group of three others in Hampshire. The foundations of the church were minimal, the walls resting on the hard natural chalk. All was well for nine hundred years, but underpinning has been carried out beneath the north transept during recent years.

The Court House south-east of the church, said to have been built about 1400, was restored by Morley Horder who purchased it in the 1920s. The river flows on the north side of the wide main

223

village street past pleasant small houses and cottages, where Glenthorne is of particular merit—an early eighteenth-century house in red and blue chequer brick with a wide eaves cornice. The doorcase architrave is in brick. It is a house of considerable quality and provides a foil to the timber-framed houses and smaller cottages in the village.

14 From East Meon to Winchester

The chalk formations extending across Hampshire have a dramatic effect on the landscape in the area of Old Winchester Hill and Butser Hill. A good place to commence exploring this countryside is from either of these hillsides, both accessible to the public. Old Winchester Hill, a nature reserve popular for summer picnics, is a vantage point from which may be seen a panorama of rounded chalk hills and blue distances.

Lanes lead through East Meon to Langrish and from Stroud to Steep, where Stoner Hill is remarkable for its wooded precipitous slopes, aptly called hangers, as the trees—most beech— seem to be literally suspended from the cliff-like sides of the hills.

Beyond the Trooper public house a lane on the right leads to Prior's Dean church, with an Early English chancel, Norman

East Meon church

doorway and little bell-turret. Inside are monuments to members of the Tichborne, Stoughton and Compton families who had interests in southern England, especially in the counties of Surrey and Hampshire.

To the north are deep 'hollow' lanes in which outcrops of malmstone may be seen grasped by the roots of trees, the branches of which bend over to shut out the sky. These delightful lanes, made by the combined usage of man and the erosion of weather, climb and descend as they turn and twist through the wooded hills and valleys to Empshott.

Empshott church is unusual and very charming. Although altered in the seventeenth and nineteenth centuries, it escaped the rigour of the Victorian restorer. The aisles may have been rebuilt—perhaps to remedy structural faults—but it is not known when this was done. The original nave arcades are beautiful examples of early thirteenth century work and the capitals of the south arcade are scalloped, stylistically slightly earlier than those to the north, which have graceful curving crockets. The nave roof trusses are cusped and with the open lantern tower beneath the spire, added in the seventeenth century, provide considerable intricacy to a fascinating timber construction. Restoration is evident, but it does not exceed the requirements of necessary repair. The south porch was moved to its present position at the west end in the seventeenth century and a chancel screen also erected. This screen, dated 1624, was moved in the 1860s and adapted to fit in the west entrance beneath the tower. Robert Aske, Lord of the Manor, led the lost cause of the Pilgrimage of Grace against Henry VIII's policy of suppression in 1537, and was suspended in chains at York where he died miserably after six days.

The magnificent brick porch with pediment of moulded brick fronting Hill Place may be seen to the east from the churchyard. Inside, a ceiling decorated with stucco reliefs of wreaths and flowers dates from the mid-seventeenth century. The house was occupied by Louise Renée de Keronalle, Duchess of Portsmouth. Lady-in-waiting to Queen Katherine de Braganza and mistress of Charles II, she bore the King a son, Charles Lennox, Duke of Richmond, in 1672.

From Empshott the Alton road passes through Selborne, a name associated with the Reverend Gilbert White, a naturalist with remarkable powers of observation. White wrote *The Natural History and Antiquities of Selborne*, a book compiled from his notes and letters which was published in 1789 when he was seventy, as a result of the enthusiasm of his brother Benjamin, a London bookseller.

Gilbert White was born in 1720 while his parents lived with his grandfather, the elder Reverend Gilbert White, vicar of Selborne, at the old vicarage which was later replaced by the present nineteenth-century building. His parents left Selborne for a time, but returned to live at The Wakes around 1729, a property which the elder Gilbert White had bequeathed to his wife Rebecca on his death in 1728. Young Gilbert lived in the house for much of his life, but not until the death in 1763 of his uncle, the Reverend Charles White, did he become its owner.

Records exist of the alterations he made to the house, notably the addition of the great parlour in 1777. However, an old house in his time, it has been suggested that the original building may date to the first half of the sixteenth century. Gilbert White's

Empshott church

parlour was a single-storey room; another section, the dining-room, was added shortly after.

Selborne Hanger, the cliff-like face of which closes the view from the garden, was described by Gilbert White as 'a vast hill of chalk, rising three hundred feet above the village; and is divided into a sheep-down, the high wood, and a long hanging wood called a hanger. The cover of this eminence is altogether beech, the most lovely of all forest trees . . .' The zigzag he and his brother John made in 1753 is still the best path to the top.

The Wakes, now a museum, houses collections relating both to the Reverend Gilbert White and Captain Lawrence Oates the Antarctic explorer. In private occupation until 1954 when the last owner died, it became possible for the Oates Trust to purchase the house using funds made up in part by public subscription, but largely from an endowment trust created by Robert Washington Oates in memory of Captain Lawrence Oates.

The older small houses and cottages in the village reflect the geology of the area. The use of pale cream malmstone with brick made of the clay from between Oakhanger and Selborne is seen everywhere. Bricks made locally are still obtainable, as well as mathematical tiles. Thatch was common, as on the cottages near The Wakes. Ferruginous sandstone—ironstone—

The Wakes, Selborne

was used for walling, galleting and also paving, in which small pieces of stone laid edgeways produced beautiful durable paths.

Selborne church, north of the Plestor—which is the village green—dates from the late twelfth century and has an imposing Norman nave arcade. The south aisle—enlarged in the late thirteenth century the Priory of Selborne as a chantry chapel—followed a gift by Ella Longspee, Countess of Warwick, to say Mass for her soul daily during her lifetime and after.

The greatest interest in the church is its connection with Gilbert White, who was for many years curate of Farringdon but later in life made a curate of Selborne. In honour of his memory a stained glass window depicts most of the birds mentioned in his writings, with St Francis of Assisi seen against a background of Selborne church and vicarage. His grave, referred to inside the church, is marked in the churchyard by a stone inscribed simply 'G.W., 26 June 1793'. A great nephew of Gilbert White carried out considerable restoration work in 1856.

Beneath a large ancient yew tree in the churchyard is a memorial stone to John Newland, trumpeter, who led the riots in 1830 seeking reform. As graphically recorded by W. H. Hudson in *Hampshire Days*, the trumpeter summoned his followers and encouraged them during an affray by blowing his trumpet.

From Selborne it is but a few miles northward to Chawton and the home of Jane Austen, where she lived for a few years until 1816 when she left for Winchester during her last illness. However, by taking the lanes across to the Fareham turnpike (A32) a visit to Farringdon, the village hall, theatre, reading-room and school known as Massey's Folly, will be of interest. Built of red brick and terracotta the Reverend T.H. Massey began building in 1870 completing the work himself with a labourer and a carpenter. Near the Folly is a timber-framed cottage called Cruck Cottage: as its name suggests, it is of cruck construction.

Chawton, at last released from the agony of fast through-traffic now diverted, instead has the parked-car problem: but nowhere is free of this—the exciting often exquisite architecture of small towns and villages is too often obscured by parked vehicles.

Jane Austen's house, L-shaped in plan, forms a courtyard at the rear where the trap house contains a carriage reputed to have belonged to Jane. A brick wing beneath three small parallel roofs forms part of the frontage, the remainder being the end elevation of a possibly older build at right angles to it. The

Jane Austen's house at Chawton

greater part of the garden front of this building is hung with mathematical tiles. The Jane Austen Museum, open to the public throughout the year, is in the house.

Chawton House and estate less than half a mile south of the village was inherited by Jane's brother Edward, on condition he changed his name to Knight. The house and stables contain late sixteenth-century work, and the church by Sir Arthur Blomfield, a rebuild in 1871 after a fire, contains a monument to Sir Richard Knight 1679, with a figure in armour and a display of trophies.

Alton has a long history and was important as a market town. It also became associated with the brewing industry, as did nearby Farnham in Surrey, the highly fertile surrounding area providing hops and barley. The long main street, now relieved of heavy traffic by a bypass, is graced by a number of eighteenth-century, and earlier, buildings. These include the grammar school of 1638, an infirmary of 1793 and also the Curtis Museum. Money and land were donated by two Alton brewers for the building of the museum, which with the old Inwood Cottage Hospital forms Crown Close.

Founded by Dr William Curtis and devoted to the work of William Curtis the botanist, as well as the rural industries and crafts of Alton, the museum also displays toys including dolls, dolls' houses and a fascinating collection of early jigsaw puzzles. Other exhibits illustrate the history of the town, the geology and natural history of the Alton area.

The Allen Gallery, in Church Street, comprises a group of recently restored sixteenth-century and eighteenth-century buildings bequeathed to the museum by William Hugh Curtis in 1957. Travelling exhibitions are held and a permanent collection includes English ceramics and silver including the Tichborne spoons and the Wickham communion set, together with paintings by W.H. Allen. Appointed Principal of Farnham School of Art in 1889, he had a considerable artistic influence in the district until the 1930s. The Curtis Museum and the Allen Gallery are part of the Hampshire County Museum Service.

Well away from the bustle of the town, Alton parish church stands in Church Street. Bullet holes to be found in the church, especially in the south doors, recall the day in December 1643 when a contingent of enlisted Royalist foot troops under Colonel Boles made a desperate stand. Alton virtually taken, Boles, with only eight men—or so it is reported—withdrew to the area of the churchyard and finally inside the church itself. Boles died in the pulpit, resolved to fight to the last.

An expression associated with the Alton has passed into general usage: 'Sweet F.A.' may now be an abbreviation of other words, but it has its origin in the particularly gruesome murder of an eight-year-old child, Fanny Adams, on 24 August 1867. The murder was extensively reported in the Press and it coincided with the issue of an unpopular tinned mutton to the Royal Navy. By a ghoulish twist 'Sweet Fanny Adams' first became a synonym for tinned mutton, then for anything worthless, and finally 'nothing at all'.

Across the A31 a lane alongside the Hen and Chickens leads to the Froyles. At Upper Froyle fine brickwork is much in evidence; a handsome brick church, with a tower built in 1722, has a nave dating from 1812. The chancel of the thirteenth century has a fourteenth-century east window with original armorial stained glass. At Froyle Place medieval origins were found concealed within Jacobean, Georgian and Victorian additions. Many smaller houses lining the village street are timber-framed, in particular Blunden House, which apart from a modern addition to the north consists of two early builds, the cross-wing to the south—possibly late sixteenth century—being an addition to an earlier hall house. Like many other houses in the village a niche in the front façade contains a statue of Our Lady, sent back to Froyle by a landowner who spent much time in Italy.

The lanes from Froyle lead for more than twelve miles over a high country of large arable fields with wooded hollows and hilltops covered with beech, past Golden Pot, the southern tip of the watershed of the Thames Valley. They lead on to Lasham Airfield, where the All England Gliding Championships are held, and across the head of the Candover valley at Axford, here

231

Steventon church

dry, to Dummer where the tiny church has an early thirteenth-century chancel and a rood canopy still in place. There are also two cottages of cruck construction in the village—Lime Tree Cottage and The Nook. Westwards is North Waltham with a village pond and thatched cottages, one of which, Rose Cottage, standing on rising ground above the pond, is of cruck construction.

The lanes beyond North Waltham lead to the scattered village of Steventon where Jane Austen was born in 1775, the youngest of the rector's seven children. She lived at the rectory for twenty-five years and wrote three of her best known books

Blunden House, Froyle

there: *Pride and Prejudice, Sense and Sensibility* and *Northanger Abbey*.

Steventon rectory was demolished long ago, and the manor house nearby is a ruin, but the church remains, probably early thirteenth century in origin with nineteenth-century alterations to the west end including the addition of a steeple. The east window was restored and the external rendering of the north and south walls of the nave and chancel renewed in 1977. Further restoration work on the tower took place in 1984. Memorials to the Austen family are in the chancel and there is a very fine fragment of a late ninth-century Saxon cross-shaft. This place is a delightful remote corner of Hampshire and the church is more satisfying and attractive than many others of greater architectural merit.

South of the old Micheldever Forest the Candovers are linked by a road from Basingstoke to Alresford and stand in a valley of particular beauty where the Itchen rises.

Preston Candover has a flint and brick church by Sir Arthur Blomfield, and just outside the village to the south is an old graveyard in which stands a small chancel, a surviving fragment of the old church.

The church at Chilton Candover, demolished in 1876, remained forgotten until 1925, when the crypt was discovered and excavated. It proved to be a Norman tunnel-vaulted rectangular structure thirty-two feet long and with an apse beyond a plain unmoulded arch—a quite remarkable find.

Brown Candover church was rebuilt on a new site in 1845. The old churchyard remains with a number of fine gravestones and monuments reflecting the former agricultural prosperity of the valley. Once one of the richest farming areas in the county, farmhouses were rebuilt in the Georgian and Victorian periods.

Lanes from the B3046 at Preston Candover lead via Upper Wield to Godsfield Farm where there is a privately owned chapel—a rare survival. It stands in the garden of a farmhouse and combines a chapel and a priest's house thought to date from the early fourteenth century. The chapel occupies the eastern section and has an east window, now blocked, three lancet windows on the south side and a north doorway. Another doorway leads to the ground floor of the priest's house which has an upper floor gained by a stair on the north side. There is a *garde-robe* attached to the upper room and a small window gives a view of the altar. The building belonged to the Knights Hospitallers who abandoned it when they moved in 1348 to their Hampshire headquarters at North Baddesley near Romsey.

The Itchen flows towards Northingon past a late nineteenth-century church built by Sir T. G. Jackson with a generous budget provided by Lord Ashburton of The Grange. The river feeds a large lake in The Grange Park where, in 1804, the Temple of Hephaestus in Athens provided a model for the portico of a mansion built for Henry Drummond, the banker.

To get the fascinating story of this area into a chronological sequence we must take a short flight south to the site of Abbotstone, a medieval village deserted in 1450, and the parish amalgamated with Itchen Stoke. The old site with foundations of houses and the church can be seen from the roadway about 350 yards east of the junction of the Itchen-Stoke road and the Abbotstone-Alresford road—it is on private property.

The mansion of the Marquis of Winchester, head of the Paulet family, remained for a time on a site now occupied by the

The Curtis Museum, Alton

235

present Abbotstone farmhouse. The great walled garden of the Paulet mansion remains.

In the 1760s the Duke of Bolton, a member of the Paulet family, drew up plans to build a great house on high ground above Abbotstone with terraced gardens sloping down to the river. However, in 1804 the property passed to the Drummonds following a foreclosure on the Marquis of Winchester. The young and very wealthy Henry Drummond then commissioned William Wilkins to take an existing seventeenth-century house at Northington, by William Samwell, and not demolish it but instead transform it into a mansion in the Greek style. Perhaps Drummond tired of the project for in 1817 he sold The Grange to Alexander Baring, a banker who later became Lord Ashburton.

Baring continued to remodel The Grange and additions were made by S.P. Cockerell and his son C.R. Cockerell in 1823-5 and 1852. Part of the original seventeenth-century house was encased within the new work.

The house was leased to George IV for a time while he followed the hounds of the fashionable Hampshire Hunt. The present fine Victorian stabling in The Grange Park was not yet built so the modest stabling then available was augmented with a fine timber-built barn. Subsequently this barn was moved and re-erected at Abbotstone Farm where after many years of agricultural use fire recently destroyed it. Following a period of decay when it looked as though the house would go beyond repair it was placed in the hands of restorers. Much scholarly work has been done on the house, particularly research on the first house reputedly by Samwell, and a brilliant paper on the house was presented to the Society of Antiquaries in 1982. The environs of the house are open to visitors.

New Alresford was 'new' in 1200 when it was laid out by Bishop de Lucy of Winchester. His reason for creating this town and others—Overton for example—was to take financial advantage by renting building plots for money rather than rents in kind. Bishop de Lucy also made the Itchen navigable from his New Alresford to Southampton, and a great feed reservoir was created by damming the River Alre to the north of the town. This is still a sizeable pond and the road to Old Alresford crosses a causeway over the dam. Watercress is extensively grown along Hampshire rivers and the Alre is no exception: many beds can be seen from this causeway.

The Reverend George Sumner lived with his wife Mary at the rectory—Old Alresford Place near Old Alresford church—and it was there that Mary Sumner founded the Mothers' Union. The house is now the Winchester Diocesan House but it was built as the rectory by Dr Hoadly and is early Georgian with later additions. Old Alresford House was built by Admiral Sir George Rodney Brydges in the mid-eighteenth century, a handsome house and open to the public.

New Alresford has three main streets, East and West Street (the A31) and Broad Street. All are cluttered with through traffic and parked vehicles to such an extent that the fine architecture of these streets cannot be appreciated. Broad Street is tree-lined and runs from the A31 to the causeway. This exceptional street, one of the best in Hampshire, has many eighteenth-century town houses—Mary Russell Mitford was born in number twenty-seven on the west side in 1787.

Fire, either accidental or deliberate, has been a curse of the town and caused damage since the twelfth century. The Royalists fired it as they fled from the Battle of Cheriton, and another fire in 1689 caused great damage. However, following a rebuild and repairs after a fire in 1736, alteration has been minimal and many buildings of the early eighteenth century survive.

Tichborne, to the south-west of New Alresford, is notable for the Tichborne dole of twelfth-century origin, and also a nine-teenth-century lawsuit. The legend of the Tichborne dole tells of Lady Marbella Tichborne, a saintly lady concerned for the poor. Old and near death she obtained a pledge from her husband enabling her to endow land for an annual gift of bread to the poor. He agreed to give as much land as she could crawl round in the time it took for a brand snatched from the fire to burn. The story tells of her circumambulating twenty acres and also of the curse she laid on the Tichborne family should the dole ever be discontinued. Strangely, misfortune has attended the family on the few occasions when this has occurred . . . The charity is still distributed on Lady Day, one gallon—an old measurement— of flour being given to every householder within a prescribed area, with half a gallon to each of their children.

The famous disputed succession in 1871 concerning the 'Tichborne Claimant' arose when Arthur Orton, a Wapping man living in Australia, claimed to be Sir Roger Tichborne the missing heir, believed drowned at sea, Sir Roger's mother, a French woman, accepted him, but other members of the family would not. After a long and expensive trial the claimant was found to be an impostor. In a subsequent trial the Crown con-victed Orton of fraud and sentenced him to fourteen years penal servitude.

The Grange, Northington

Alresford

240

Tichborne has many thatched cottages dotted along its lanes: one of particular interest, Park View Cottage, is timber-framed and the central roof truss is of cruck construction. The church has a tower of brick dated 1703 and the chancel is of considerable interest. It dates from a period of transition when Saxon building methods continued in use, as yet not entirely replaced by those of the Normans.

There is Norman influence in the regular ashlar work, both in the window jambs and heads and also in the pilaster strips or buttresses. The north and south windows however, double splayed in the Saxon manner, retain a mid-wall slab pierced to form the aperture. After the Dissolution, the church was divided to provide a mortuary chapel for the Tichborne family, who were leading Roman Catholics. The small chapel has many memorials: the finest, commemorating Sir Benjamin Tichborne who died in 1621, has alabaster effigies of him, his wife and children. Another commemorates Richard Tichborne who died at the age of 'one yeare six months and two dies' by drowning following a gypsy's curse.

The Battle of Cheriton was fought on 29 March 1644 at the head of a dry valley between Cheriton village and Cheriton Wood. About twenty thousand troops confronted each other, under the Parliamentarian commander Sir William Waller—who spent the night before the battle at Hinton Ampner House—and Lords Forth and Hopton for the Crown. It was a decisive and bloody victory for the Parliamentarians, won by disciplined troops against an impetuous and ill-timed attack by Royalist cavalry. The scene of the battle, which seems very small considering the numbers involved, is marked by a monolith set up by public subscription.

William Cobbett described Cheriton as 'a little hard, iron village, where all seems to be as old as the hills that surround it'. A charming place, through which the infant Itchen flows dividing into several branches crossed by bridges, it has a thirteenth-century church standing on a mound west of the village which is said by some writers to be a pre-Christian sacred site.

Two and a half miles south of Cheriton through Beauworth a public house and restaurant—formerly the Fox and Hounds but now Millburys, so-called after the barrows nearby—should be visited to see the large donkey treadwheel. North-west from here across Gander Down and beyond Cheesefoot Head, where the Admiralty had a semaphore station on Telegraph Hill, is the village of Chilbomb and a small Norman church along a lane below Deacon Hill. Inside is an iron hook above the altar, upon which hung the pyx containing the Eucharistic Host.

Returning to the Itchen and the villages along the river west of New Alresford, Ovington is a delightful place where streams meet. The church is Victorian and the Bush Inn, with gardens bordering the stream, is not old but very attractive both inside and out. A path leads from the inn across the river to Itchen Stoke, where the vicar, one Reverend Charles Conybeare, built a church at his own expense. The building is tall and in a flamboyant Gothic style that looks French—indeed it is said to have been inspired by the Sainte Chapelle in Paris.

The use of flint for walling is common in and near the chalk regions, but brick or stone was usually used to form corners and openings. At Itchen Stoke however there is a small flint house which was formerly the village school, built with exceptionally large flints which alone form substantial corners.

Westward from Itchen Stoke, Itchen Abbas has developed as a residential area of large houses set in wooded gardens. The church is in a Victorian-Norman style and was in the process of being built when Charles Kingsley visited the village and enjoyed fishing the river nearby. He stayed at The Plough—now rebuilt—and wrote *The Water Babies*. The river may have prompted some passages in the book.

The Liberal statesman, Lord Grey of Fallodon, foreign minister from 1905-14 had a 'retreat' at Itchen Abbas and wrote a book of reminiscences of his youth by the river. His cottage was burnt down in 1923. The grave of John Hughes (ratcatcher) in the churchyard recalls the extent to which capital punishment was used a little more than a century and a half ago. He was hanged for horse stealing, and although of little consolation to him, he was the last person to receive the death penalty for that offence.

A lane past Itchen Abbas church crosses the river to Avington and Avington Park, where Charles II found lodging for Nell Gwynne: the owner, after all, was George Rodney Brydges, Groom of the Bedchamber. The Prebendary of Winchester, Thomas Ken, 'would not give poor Nelly lodging.' Avington Park was remodelled in the early eighteenth century, perhaps by John James. It has a west façade with two four-bay pilastered wings flanking a centre portico of wood. The church at the edge of the park is one of the finest of its date in the country. It was built for the Marchioness of Carnarvon, who died in 1768 and did not live to see its completion although the main fabric of the building was probably finished in her lifetime. The interior is superb and has box pews, and a three-decker pulpit with canopy as well as a nineteenth-century barrel-organ which plays hymn tunes and chants.

South-east of Avington is Hampage Wood and the Gospel Oak. This wood remains as a reminder of a king's grudging gift of timber from the wood to the wily Bishop of Walkelin for his cathedral at Winchester.

The church at Easton is remarkable for its late Norman architecture and dates from 1200. The chancel and apse are exceptional for the beauty of the vaulting and the arch between them, the capitals in this arch being quite exquisite. There was some restoration by Woodyer in the 1860s and he was responsible for the rather odd shingled upper section of the tower.

A rector of Easton, William Barlow, was the son of Agatha, once a nun. An inscription on a monument recalls that she married a bishop and had five daughters who married five bishops—one was Herbert Westfayling who was 'never betrayed into laughter'.

Martyr Worthy includes a group of timber-framed and thatched cottages now restored and modernized and also a remarkable pseudo-medieval timber-framed house. St Swithun's has a late Norman nave with tall north and south doorways which are deceptively narrow and which tempt a brief thought that they may be of Saxon origin—but they are Norman and late at that. The bell-turret and apse date to a mid-nineteenth-century rigorous restoration. The village street, or lane, slopes down past the church to a footpath and bridge over the river, which is here denuded of bankside tree growth to please the fishermen but with the lush growth of summer is no less beautiful.

Abbots Worthy and Kings Worthy stand near the new junction of the A33 (T) and the A34 (T) and the road along the Itchen valley from New Alresford. Modern housing northward from here extends from the outskirts of Winchester to some three and a half miles from the centre. The small group of houses around the large church of Kings Worthy are of interest, one or two of which are timber-framed.

The church, although much restored, makes a pleasing architectural composition enhanced by the fourteenth-century tower.

At Headbourne Worthy the church contains one of Hampshire's priceless architectural possessions—a Saxon stone rood of a kind unsurpassed in Europe. Much of the Saxon fabric of the church remains: there is long and short work at the angles of chancel and nave, and Saxon lesenes on the north wall of the nave and the south wall of the chancel. Settlement obviously caused trouble in the past and several medieval buttresses were added. The Saxon chancel was extended in the thirteenth century and the south-west tower and tall porch against the west wall of the nave date from the sixteenth century.

When G.E. Street restored the church in 1865–6 he took down the Saxon north wall of the nave, also the south wall of the chancel, and renewed the foundations. Stones were numbered and replaced. The west wall of the nave—with a particularly good Saxon door opening—and the rood above, were fortunately not in need of attention. The rood has similarities to those at Breamore and Romsey and depicts the hand of God appearing in a cloud above Christ. It also includes large figures of the Virgin and St John. Disastrously, and ironically, the bigotry of the age led to the mutilation of this remarkable and very pious work sometime following the year 1547 when Edward VI ordered the destruction of all crucifixes. Only a silhouette remains, the relief of the sculpture having been almost chiselled away, but even in its mutilated state it is still an impressive work.

My picture of Hampshire ends here, two miles from Winchester Cathedral where it began. Spiced with a little history and geology, it indulges my interest in architecture excluding all but a passing reference to modern developments. A personal impression is offered formed with words and drawings intended to be but a glimpse of a large and beautiful county.

Glossary

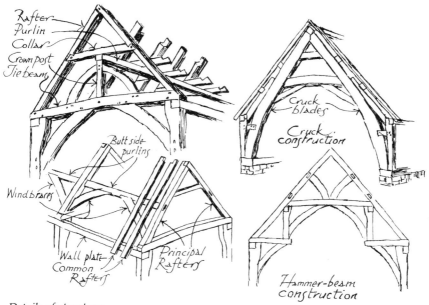

Rafter
Purlin
Collar
Crown post
Tie beam

Butt side
purlins

Wind braces

Wall plate
Common
Rafters

Principal
Rafters

Cruck
blades

Cruck
construction

Hammer-beam
construction

Details of structure

Aisle: from the Latin ala—a wing. An outer, lateral division of a building appended to the main body.

Alabaster: gypsum (sulphate of lime). A stone principally taken from Derbyshire not unlike marble in appearance. It weathers badly and is unsuitable for external work. It is easy to work and allows a high degree of polish and detailed finish. Extensively used in church monuments in the later Middle Ages.

Apse: the termination of an architectural unit, such as a church, showing in plan as a half circle, a half ellipse or a half polygon.

Arcade: a row of free-standing posts (arcade posts) or piers (arcade piers), supporting an upper structure, usually of arches, or in a timber-framed building, an arcade plate (q.v.). A blind arcade is the same but stands against a wall.

Arcade Plate: a horizontal timber passing across the heads of the posts in an arcade.

Architrave: in Classical architecture it is a member of the upper structure immediately above the column and below the frieze (q.v.)

Baluster: a vertical member of an identical series supporting a coping or handrail and thus forming a balustrade.

Bargate Stone: a sandstone found in the Godalming area, of a warm brown colour caused by the presence of iron. It can be built in courses, but is more often used as rubble stone.

Barge-Board: a board, one of a pair, usually, but not necessarily, carved. With its face in a vertical plane it is attached along the whole length of the gable end of a roof and follows the terminal edge of the roof covering.

Bay: a division in a framed building limited by the principal posts (q.v.) and the principal roof trusses (q.v.). It is also an external lateral division defined by the fenestration.

Bond: the arrangement in which bricks are laid. The three most common are: Header bond in which every course is laid with bricks placed end on; English bond in which the courses of header bricks alternate with courses of stretchers, i.e. bricks laid lengthways; Flemish bond in which every course is laid with alternate headers and stretchers arranged so that headers occur centrally between stretchers in alternate courses.

Brace: in a framed structure, can be straight, curved or ogee. It is set to strengthen the angle between two other members. Can be used in compression, or in later work, tension.

Build: a currently accepted noun derived from the verb to build, used to refer to a construction, or part of a construction, erected at any one time. A complete building may comprise several builds.

Burgage: a property held in a town involving a fixed money rent.

Butt Side Purlin: a purlin placed between principal rafters, in fact not butted, but jointed by mortice and tenon (q.v.).

Caen Stone: a limestone from the Caen region of Normandy in France.

Camber: in a tie-beam, slight curve or arch so that the centre is higher than the ends.

Capital: of a column, can be carved or be comprised of mouldings.

Canopy of grace—Celure: panelled, or specially decorated area of a church roof above a rood-screen (q.v.).

Carstone: hard stone from the Lower Greensand, an iron oxide content gives it a dark brown colour. Suitable for use as rubble also for galleting (q.v.)

Casement: window hinged on one vertical edge, opens either inwards or outwards.

Centre Purlin: *see* Diagram.

Chamfer: a bevel formed by the removal of the angle of a squared timber or stone.

246

Chancel: a part of a church east of the nave and containing the altar.

Chancel Arch: an arch standing between the nave and the chancel.

Chantry Chapel: a chapel attached to, or within, a church endowed for the singing of Masses for the soul of the founder or others designated by him.

Choir: the part of the church where the services are sung.

Cladding: material used externally as a covering to a wall.

Close Studding: vertical intermediate timbers in a wall of a framed structure placed little more than their own width apart, usually for decoration.

Clunch: hard form of chalk capable of being carved and used as a building stone.

Coade Stone: very durable artificial stone of unknown composition used for casting architectural ornament, popular from about 1770 until around 1836.

Collar-beam: *see* Diagram.

Collar Purlin: synonymous with centre purlin, *see* Diagram.

Colonnade: row of columns supporting a superstructure, *see* arcade.

Continuous Jetty: a jetty (q.v.) running along the full length of the side of a framed house.

Corbel: a projection provided to support a weight.

Corinthian: a Classical order with fluted column and carved capital employing acanthus leaf motif.

Cornice: upper projecting section of an entablature (q.v.) in Classical architecture; also decorated termination to the top of a wall.

Cross Passage: or screens passage, crosses the lower end of a hall giving access at front and rear, also with entrances into the hall and doorways to pantry, buttery and passage to kitchen.

Cross Potent: a cross with bars across the ends of the arms.

Crosswing: a wing with an upper storey set transversely to the main structure of a house.

Crownpost: *see* Diagram.

Cruck Construction: *see* Diagram.

Cupola: a Classical feature, a domed turret crowning a roof.

Decorated: historical period of English Gothic architecture from *c.* 1272-1377.

Dentil Moulding: comprises a row of blocks retangular or square in section placed below a cornice. A feature of Classical origin.

Diaper: in brickwork the formation of an all-over pattern, often diamond, by using bricks of a different colour to those of the main wall surface.

Dog-Tooth: decoration consisting of a row of small pyramidal forms cut to represent four leaves.

Doric: a Classical order, its most famous use is to be found in the Athenian Parthenon.

Dormer: a window set vertically in a roof, with its own roof.

Dressings: work placed around openings, e.g. doors and windows, often of a material superior to that of the main structure, to provide a finish.

Dutch Gable: *see* Gable.

Early English: the first period of English Gothic architecture following the Transitional period, from about 1189 until 1272 during the reigns of Richard I, John, and Henry III.

Eaves Cornice: projecting upper termination to a wall, moulded or carved, set at the over-hang of a pitched roof.

Entablature: the whole of the horizontal members above a column in Classical architecture, comprises architrave, frieze and cornice.

First Floor Hall: principal room in a medieval hall house raised to the first floor.

Floored: containing an upper floor, or to have received an inserted floor as a later addition.

Framed: constructed of timber, jointed together to form an open framework that is infilled with other material.

Frieze: horizontal division beneath the cornice (q.v.) in Classical architecture, often moulded or carved.

Gable: triangular area of a wall closing the end of a ridged roof. A Dutch gable has a curved profile rising in front of the roof and is crowned by a pediment (q.v.). A shaped gable is the same but lacks the pediment.

Galleried: containing an upper open passage across the front giving access to a series of rooms.

Galleting, Garneting: small chips of stone or flint set into wide mortar joints while still wet to save the mortar from the action of weather. Also has a decorative purpose as internal use has been found.

Garderobe: a lavatory or privy.

Gothic Revival: interest in medieval art that commenced in the eighteenth century and flourished in the nineteenth. In architecture it produced work that simulated the appearance of the original, but not the spirit.

Gothick: term applied to fanciful interpretations of Gothic styles.

Half-Timbering: synonymous with timber-framed and framed (q.v.).

Hall: principal room in a medieval house, later became of less importance and now survives as the area into which a main entrance opens.

Hammer-Beam Roof: form of roof capable of covering a width comparable to that of an aisled building. Arcade posts (q.v.) are dispensed with by the use of short bracketed beams (hammer-beams) at wall-plate (q.v.) level that support posts (hammer-posts) set beneath the purlins.

Header: *see* Bond.

Hip: sloping section of roof closing the end of a building and extending from an end tie-beam, or wall plate, (full hip), or from a collar beam (half hip) to the apex or gable.

Ionic: Classical order distinguished by a voluted capital.
Ironstone: synonymous with carstone.

Jetty: projection formed by the extension of floor joists so that an upper floor overhangs a lower.

Keep: strongly fortified tower in a castle designed to be both a residence and a place of last resort in case of attack.

Lancet: narrow window opening with a pointed head of the Transitional and Early English styles (q.v.).
Lap: joint formed by one member overlapping a part of another.
Lesene: associated with Saxon architecture, flat or shallow projection attached to a stone wall, said to be a decoration originating from timber construction, but may also be intended to add strength to the wall.
Lunette: as applied to a window, half-moon shaped.

Malmstone: a soft sandstone from the upper greensand which varies in colour from grey to almost white.
Manor: unit of land and its associated social group managed under the authority of a lord of the manor.
Mathematical Tiles: so made that when they are hung on battens, or embedded in plaster, they can be pointed up to be indistinguishable from brickwork.
Merstham Stone: synonymous with Reigate stone and firestone, a sandstone favoured by masons because of its easy working qualities, similar to Caen stone (q.v.) but it weathers very badly.
Mortice and Tenon: most common joint in English carpentry since the Romanesque period, *c.* twelfth century, in which the tongue (tenon) on one section is inserted into the socket (mortice) in the other.
Mullion: vertical dividing bar in a window opening.

Nave: in a church, the main body of the building for the use of the laity.
Newel: central post around which a stair is constructed; or the principal posts in a staircase between which the balusters and baluster rails are placed.

Ogee: a double curve, concave passing to convex.
Open hall: in a medieval house, a single storey living space open to the roof with a fire on a hearth without a chimney.
Oriel: bay window extending upwards from the ground, or supported at a higher level by brackets.

Orné: fanciful style based upon an imaginary, idealized, conception of rustic architecture.

Outshot, Outshut: a lean-to or extension at the rear of a house.

Palladian: style of architecture based upon the work and writings of Andrea Palladio 1518-80.

Pantry: from Old French *paneterie,* food store.

Parapet: low wall to afford protection from a drop, on a bridge or house top.

Parclose Screen: divides a side chapel from the rest of the church.

Pediment: triangular shape above the entablature of a Classical portico or opening.

Perpendicular: historical period of English Gothic architecture from *c.* 1377-1547.

Pilaster: shallow pier of rectangular section attached to a wall.

Piscina: basin placed near the altar for washing the chalice, set in the wall and often the subject of decorative treatment, provided with a drain that soaks away within the wall.

Principal Posts: main upright timbers that extend to the full height of a timber frame.

Portico: Classical feature at an entrance composed of columns, either attached or detached, and supporting an entablature (q.v.) often with a pediment (q.v.)

Purlin: centre purlin, side purlin, *see* Diagram.

Puthole: or putlock hole, in a wall to take the putlock or short horizontal bar of a scaffold, the holes may be filled, closed with a stone, or left open.

Pyx: a receptacle in which the Eucharistic Host is kept.

Quatrefoil: applied to an aperture, or arch, containing cusps that break it into four leaf shapes. Trefoil and cinquefoil have three and five divisions respectively.

Quoin: dressed corner stone of a wall.

Rafter: *see* Diagram.

Reigate Stone: synonymous with Merstham Stone (q.v.)

Reredos: structure of both decorative and religious content behind and above—but not attached to—an altar.

Roll Moulding: a rounded moulding approaching a complete circular section to a greater or lesser degree.

Rood: crucifix or cross. Rood-loft, a gallery above a rood-screen which is placed between the nave and the chancel.

Sandstone: stone composed of consolidated sand. Varies considerably in colour and durability.

Sans-Purlin: a roof in which there are no purlins.

Sarsen Stone: synonymous with heathstone and greyweather. Sandstone boulders found on, or just beneath, the heaths, remnants conveyed from once more complete layers of sandstone. From the word saracen—a stranger.

Scratch Dial: mass dial, a small sundial with a central hole to take a gnomon, of pre-Reformation date and used by a priest to determine the canonical hours.

Screens Passage: synonymous with cross-passage.

Sedilia: seats for the celebrant and two assistants on the south side of the chancel of a church.

Shaped Gable: *see* Gable.

Shingle: cleft oak tile, cut with a thick upper edge and a thin lower one—used on roofs and walls.

Shaft: in medieval architecture a slender column; in Classical architecture the member of a column between the capital and the base.

Spandrel: triangular space between the outer curve of an arch and the rectangle formed by the mouldings enclosing it.

Squint: hole cut in a wall to give a view of the main altar.

Stiff-Leaf: early form of carved leaf developed through the Transitional period (q.v.) and perfected in the Early English (q.v.)

Strut: intermediary roof timber supporting a beam; it may be vertical (queen strut), or set at an angle (angle strut) to support a purlin when the collar is omitted.

Studs—Studding: intermediate vertical timbers set in a wall frame.

Tenon: *see* Mortice and Tenon.

Tie-beam: *see* Diagram.

Tile-Hanging: wall covering of overlapping tiles hung on battens, may be used over a brick or framed wall as a protection against weather, or in the latter case as cladding.

Timber-Framing: *see* Framed.

Transept: north and south transverse arms in a church with a cruciform plan.

Trefoil: *see* Quatrefoil.

Tuscan Order: a modified form of the Doric order (q.v.).

Turnpike: began with an Act in 1663 allowing Justices of the Peace to erect gates (turnpikes) and charge tolls for the purpose of improving and maintaining roads.

Transitional: period of change, notably that from Norman Romanesque to English Gothic.

Truss: principal framework of a roof, designed to support other members, and set at bay (q.v.) intervals.

Voussoir: a brick or wedge-shaped stone forming one of the units of an arch.

Wall-Plate: horizontal timber at the top of a wall (stone, brick or framed) from which the rafters are pitched.

Wealden House: type of hall house with continuous eaves in which the end bays only are jettied forward thus creating the illusion of a recessed centre. Most common in the Weald, but of wide distribution elsewhere.

Weather-Boarding: horizontal overlapping feather-edged boards covering a framed wall.

Wind-Braces: strengthening timbers placed between a side purlin and a principal rafter. May be curved or straight or decoratively treated. *See* Diagram.

Bibliography

Alcock, N. W., *Cruck Construction: an introduction and catalogue.* CBA Research Report (The Council for British Archaeology) 1981

Armstrong, J. R., *Traditional Buildings Accessible to the Public* (EP Publishing) 1979

Balfour, Alan, *Portsmouth* (Studio Vista) 1970

Benham, Revd W., DD, *Winchester Cathedral* (Isbister) 1898

Brunskill, R. W., *Illustrated Handbook of Vernacular Architecture* (Faber) 1970

Capes, Revd W. W., *Scenes of Rural Life in Hampshire Among the Manors of Bramshott* (Macmillan) 1901

Church, A. H., MA, FRS, *The Chemistry of Paints and Painting* (Seeley Service & Co) 1892

Clapham, Sir Alfred, *English Romanesque Architecture* (2 vols: *Before the Conquest*, 1930; *After the Conquest*, 1932. Clarendon Press)

Clifton-Taylor, Alec. *The Pattern of English Building* (Faber) 1972

Clifton-Taylor, Alec, *The Cathedrals of England* (Thames & Hudson) 1967

Clifton-Taylor, Alec, and Brunskill, R. W., *English Brickwork* (Ward Lock) 1977

Cobbett, William, *Rural Rides*, 1830 (Penguin Books Edition, 1967)

Cox, Charles, (revised Jowitt, 1949) *Hampshire: The Little Guides* (Methuen) 1949

Crawford, O. G. S., FSA, and Keiller, A., FSA, FGS, *Wessex from the Air* (Clarendon Press) 1928

Crook, John, *A History of The Pilgrims' School* (Phillimore) 1981

Defoe, Daniel, *A Tour of England and Wales* (Everyman) 1927

Dugdale, William, *The Monasticon Anglicanum.* Abridged English version, London, 1692

Dutton, R., *Hampshire* (Batsford) 1970

Fiennes, Celia, *The Journey of Celia Fiennes* (Cressett Press) 1947

Goodwin, Revd G. N., *The Civil War in Hampshire 1642–5* and *the Story of Basing House* (Henry March Gilbert & Son and John & Edward Bumpus Ltd) 1904

Gunnis, Rupert, *Dictionary of British Sculptors 1660–1851* (Abbey Library) 1951

Harris, R., *Discovering Timber Buildings* (Shire Publications) 1978

Herringham, Christine, J., *The Book of the Art of Cennino Cennini: A contemporary practice treatise of quato-centro painting translated from Italian* (Allen & Unwin Ltd) 1899

Hewitt, Cecil, A., *English Historic Carpentry* (Phillimore) 1980

Horn, W., and Born, C., *The Barns of the Abbey of Beaulieu at its Grange of Great Coxwell and Beaulieu St Leonards* (University of California Press) 1965

Hudson, W. H., *Hampshire Days* (OUP paperback) 1980

Hughes, Michael, *The Small Towns of Hampshire* (Hampshire Archaeological Committee.)

Kalokyris, Konstantin, *The Byzantine Wall Paintings of Crete* (English translation Red Dust Inc.) 1973

Kitchen, Dean G. W., *Winchester* (Historic Towns Series)

Laurie, A. P., MA, D.Sc., *The Materials of the Painter's Craft* (Foulis) 1910

Lloyd, N., *History of the English House* (Architectural Press (reprint)) 1975

Mason, R. T., *Framed Buildings of England* (Coach Publishing House Ltd.) 1972

Meirion-Jones, Gwyn I., *The Wakes, Selborne* (The Oates Memorial Library & Museum and the Gilbert White Museum) 1979

Melville, R. V., M.Sc., and Freshley, E. C., B.Sc., Ph.D., *British Regional Geology: Hampshire Basin and adjoining areas*

Merryfield, Mary P., *The Art of Fresco Painting* (Alec Tiranti Ltd. (reprint)) 1952

Murray's Handbook, *Hampshire* 1898

O'Dell, Noreen, *The River Itchen* (Paul Cave Publications Ltd.) 1977

O'Dell, Noreen, *The River Test* (Paul Cave Publications Ltd.) 1979

O'Dell, Noreen, *Portrait of Hampshire* (Hale) 1979

Page, William, FSA, (editor) *The Victoria County History of Hampshire and the Isle of Wight* (University of London Institute of Historical Research. Reprint Dawson) 1973

Park, David, *The Romanesque Paintings of All Saints' Church, Witley, Surrey* (Surrey Archaeological Society Collections, vol 74) 1983

Pevsner, N., and Lloyd, David, *Hampshire and the Isle of Wight*, Buildings of England Series (Penguin) 1967

Read, Moutray, *Highways and Byways in Hampshire* (Macmillan) 1928

Richardson, Sir Alfred, *The Old Inns of England* (Batsford) 1934

Rickman, Thomas, FSA, *An attempt to discriminate the styles of architecture in England from the Conquest to the Reformation* (John Henry and James Parker) 1819

Rigold, S. E., MA, FSA, *Portchester Castle, Hampshire* (HMSO) 1965

Rouse, Dr E. Clive, *Discovering Wall Paintings* (Shire Publications) 1968

Ruskin, John, LLD, DCL, *Modern Painters* vol 4 (George Allen) 1897

Salzman, L. F., FSA, *Building in England down to 1540* (Clarendon Press) 1952

Taylor, H. M., and Taylor, Joan, *Anglo-Saxon Architecture* vols 1 and 2 (CUP) 1965

Taylor, H. M., *Anglo-Saxon Architecture* vol 3 (CUP) 1978

Varley, Revd Telford, MA, B.Sc., *Hampshire* (A. & C. Black) 1909

Vesey-Fitzgerald, Brian, *Hampshire and the Isle of Wight* (Hale) 1949

Warren, William Thorn, *Warren's Guide to Winchester* (Warren & Son) *c*.1920

Watcher, John, *The Towns of Roman Britain* (Batsford) 1974

Wickham, C. T., *The Story of Twyford School* (Warren & Son), 1909

Wight, J., *Brick Building in England* (John Baker) 1972

Willis, Revd R., MA., FRS, *Architectural History of Winchester Cathedral* (reprint by The Friends of Winchester Cathedral) 1980

Wood, M., *The English Medieval House* (Ferndale Editions) 1981

Ziegler, Philip, *The Black Death* (Collins) 1969

Other sources of valuable information

The Dictionary of National Biography (Oxford University Press)

Ordnance Survey and British Geological Survey Maps

Guide books produced by individual churches and other buildings open to the public

Tourist Bureaux were very helpful in supplying local information and guide books

Index

261

270